The Italian Diaspora in South Africa

This book investigates the experiences of second- and third-generation Italians living in South Africa, exploring how nostalgia for Italy influences their sense of identity and belonging.

The Italian community in South Africa is a unique diaspora, with a complex history, including roots in Italian colonial activities in Africa, and in World War II. This book looks at how the descendants of these early migrants take pride in being Italian and value the Italian language. The descendants also ascribe much importance to their family roots and have often created a romanticized image of Italy, mostly based on childhood vacation visits. The longing for an imaginary idealized version of Italy is closely linked to their wider search for a sense of identity and belonging against the backdrop of South African society, currently still grappling with its own multicultural identity.

Interdisciplinary by design, this book draws on insights from both cultural studies and psychology in order to shine a light on an important and understudied diasporic community. The book will be of interest to scholars from across migration studies and the humanities in general.

Maria Chiara Marchetti-Mercer is Professor of Psychology at the School of Human and Community Development, University of the Witwatersrand, Johannesburg, South Africa.

Anita Virga is Associate Professor at the School of Literature, Language and Media, University of the Witwatersrand, Johannesburg, South Africa.

Routledge Studies in Development, Mobilities and Migration

This series is dedicated to the growing and important area of mobilities and migration, particularly through the lens of international development. It promotes innovative and interdisciplinary research targeted at a global readership. The series welcomes submissions from established and junior authors on cutting-edge and high-level research on key topics that feature in global news and public debate.

These include the so called European migration crisis; famine in the Horn of Africa; riots; environmental migration; development-induced displacement and resettlement; livelihood transformations; people-trafficking; health and infectious diseases; employment; South-South migration; population growth; children's wellbeing; marriage and family; food security; the global financial crisis; drugs wars; and other contemporary crisis.

Mapping Southern Routes of Migrant Women
A Case Study of Chile
Sondra Cuban

Migration and Development in Southern Europe and South America
Edited by Maria Damilakou and Yannis G. S. Papadopoulos

Border Crossings and Mobilities on Screen
Edited by Ruxandra Trandafoiu

Refugee Resilience and Adaptation in the Middle East
Reclaiming Agency in the Informal Economies of Lebanon and Jordan
Edited by Haya Al-Dajani, Maysa Baroud, and Nasser Yassin

The Italian Diaspora in South Africa
Nostalgia, Identity, and Belonging in the Second and Third Generations
Maria Chiara Marchetti-Mercer and Anita Virga

For more information about this series, please visit: www.routledge.com/
Routledge-Studies-in-Development-Mobilities-and-Migration/book-series/
RSDM

The Italian Diaspora in South Africa

Nostalgia, Identity, and Belonging in the Second and Third Generations

Maria Chiara Marchetti-Mercer and Anita Virga

Routledge
Taylor & Francis Group
LONDON AND NEW YORK

First published 2023
by Routledge
4 Park Square, Milton Park, Abingdon, Oxon OX14 4RN

and by Routledge
605 Third Avenue, New York, NY 10158

Routledge is an imprint of the Taylor & Francis Group, an informal business

© 2023 Maria Chiara Marchetti-Mercer and Anita Virga

The right of Maria Chiara Marchetti-Mercer and Anita Virga to be
identified as authors of this work has been asserted in accordance with
sections 77 and 78 of the Copyright, Designs and Patents Act 1988.

Trademark notice: Product or corporate names may be
trademarks or registered trademarks, and are used only for
identification and explanation without intent to infringe.

British Library Cataloguing-in-Publication Data
A catalogue record for this book is available from the British Library

ISBN: 978-1-032-21126-8 (hbk)
ISBN: 978-1-032-21128-2 (pbk)
ISBN: 978-1-003-26688-4 (ebk)

DOI: 10.4324/9781003266884

Typeset in Times New Roman
by Deanta Global Publishing Services, Chennai, India

This book is dedicated to our children, Connor, Francesca and Zofia, second-generation Italians born in South Africa. May their italianità always provide them with a sense of home and belonging.

Contents

Acknowledgements

This research would not have been possible without financial support for the field work and the work needed towards the publication of this book. We would like to thank the Com.It.Es. of Cape Town, who recognized the importance of this work for the Italian community in South Africa. We would also like to thank the Mellon Foundation and the Faculty of Humanities of the University of the Witwatersrand for their support, which allowed us to carry out the fieldwork, as well as to finalize the publication of the book.

Three very special people assisted us in different phases of this project: Julia Martinelli, who transcribed all the interviews in a very professional and efficient manner; Sonto Madonsela, who collaborated with the data analysis; and Idette Noomé, our language editor, whose helpful suggestions added much value to the final version of this book.

We want to acknowledge various Italian institutions in South Africa for their interest in and encouragement for our project, namely the Embassy of Italy in Pretoria, the General Consulate of Italy in Johannesburg, the Consulate of Italy in Cape Town, and the Italian Institute of Culture in Pretoria.

We hope that through this work, the Italian community in South Africa may become more visible in the international arena, both academic and non-academic. Their resilience, hard work, and creativity have added much to the social and economic fabric of South African society over the years. In particular, we thank all our participants for their generosity in agreeing to share their life stories with us and for the depth of their reflections. This book would not have been possible without them.

Finally – but very importantly – we would like to express our gratitude to our families for their patience and support while we were writing this book.

1 Situating our work

Introduction

Acclaimed South African poet Don Mattera, of Italian and Xhosa descent, recalling his Italian grandfather, Paolo Mattera, who came to South Africa from Ischia, in the Gulf of Naples, in 1904, wrote about his grandfather's and his own relationship to Italy:

> Sometimes he reminisced about his country and his people, and their history of war and peace. But so thick, like a swelling river, flowed the music of his land in his veins, that when he sang a lump instantly came to his throat. The choking was gentle. I traced tears of longing and nostalgia in his half-blind eyes. Through them I virtually lived in the farm cottage in his native Italy, and walked among the olive trees eating as I sang. It was my feet that crushed the grapes to make wine, my hands that ground the wheat and harvested potatoes. Even my blood was shed in the long vendettas. I became one with them who I had never seen or touched or spoken to.
>
> (Mattera, 2009, p. 29)

These moving words connect a first-generation immigrant, Paolo Mattera, to his third-generation descendant, Don, and reveal many of the themes we explore in this book relating to identity, belonging, and nostalgia. Mattera's warm and loving description captures the very essence of this book, epitomising the relationship between descendants of Italian immigrants with Italy.

Research into identity and belonging

A few years ago, the two authors of this book came together as academics from diverse disciplines in the Humanities working at the same university with a common interest in the experiences of Italian migrants living in South Africa. We are both Italian-born women who migrated to South Africa at very different times in our lives and under different political dispensations. We both have a very particular involvement in the Italian community in South

DOI: 10.4324/9781003266884-1

Africa, and we both have an interest in migration, albeit from different theoretical perspectives – one more therapeutic and the other more literary. We believe that this personal positioning was crucial in the choice of our research focus, as well as in how we wrote this book.

We initially wanted to focus on the experiences of second-generation Italian migrants and their sense of *italianità*. However, as we explain in more detail below, we soon decided to broaden the scope of our investigation to include third-generation immigrant participants. Moreover, as our research progressed, we realized that we could not look just at participants' sense of an Italian identity. We also had to reflect on their relationship with the land of their birth, South Africa. Consequently, as our project unfolded, we discovered that the question of "belonging" that is often highlighted in migration literature (see, for example, Castles & Davidson, 2020; Gilmartin, 2008; Skrbiš, 2008; Skrbiš et al., 2007) is, in fact, a significant aspect of the stories of the descendants of the original Italian immigrants to South Africa who participated in our study. This also led us to reflect on different aspects of what may be seen as an inherited nostalgia which often leads to a longing, either imagined or actual, to "return" to Italy. We then also explored how this nostalgia is linked to participants' overall sense of belonging, which emerged as a *Leitmotiv* in the psychological experience of the South African part of the Italian diasporas.

Our main objective was to investigate the experiences of the descendants of those who originally immigrated to South Africa in terms of their identity and belonging, bringing together our two diverse theoretical lenses as researchers, reflected in our academic backgrounds, namely family therapy and the psychology of migration on the one hand, and Italian and cultural studies on the other.

We do not claim to represent the overall experiences of all South African-born second- and third-generation Italians. The participants who were willing to participate in this study by sharing their stories with us had already developed their connection with their Italian origins. There may be many more people living in South Africa who have a very different experience of their *italianità* and a different relationship with Italy. However, we believe that this book will provide a meaningful glimpse into the Italian diaspora in South Africa.

The Italian diaspora in South Africa

Historically, Italy has long been a country subject to emigration. Large numbers of migrants left the country soon after unification in 1861, and outward migration has continued since then. However, in recent decades, Italy has also become a place of immigration. Especially with the fall of Albania in the 1990s, Italy has become the destination of a large number of people who leave their own countries to reach the Italian shores, usually by crossing the Mediterranean Sea.

In response to this migratory tradition, a large body of academic work has focused on Italians who left the land of their birth for other countries in search of a better life for themselves and their descendants. Second- and third-generation Italians have been widely researched in different parts of the Italian diasporic experience, especially in North America, Australia, and other parts of Europe. Arguably, the best-known research on this topic focuses on Italian immigration to the United States, mainly because of the large and important migratory flow to that destination in the 19th and 20th centuries, and because of the importance of the United States in the world today (see, for example, the studies by Gabaccia, 2000; Gans, 1982; Haller, 2011; Mangione & Morreale, 1992; Piccoli, 2014). In Australia, Baldassar (1999, 2011), Sala (2017), and Sala and Baldassar (2017a, 2017b) have produced pioneering work on the role of the family in the process of ethnic transmission in younger generations. More recently, Marino (2019, 2020, 2021) has also described some second- and third-generation Italians' experiences in Australia. European researchers such as Wessendorf (2007, 2008, 2010, 2016) have described the phenomenon of a "roots migration" amongst Swiss-born Italians.

By comparison, very limited academic research has so far been conducted on the psychological and social experiences of the Italian community in South Africa, with the exception of work by Buranello (2009), Giuliani-Balestrino (1995), Macioti and Zaccai (2006), and Milanese (2002). This lacuna may be ascribed partly to the fact that the number of Italian immigrants who came to South Africa is relatively low, compared to the numbers of Italian migrants to other countries, and partly to the complex political history of their chosen country of destination. During the apartheid years (1948 to 1994), there was tension between the Italian community living in South Africa and Italians in Italy, because the mere fact of living in South Africa was seen as a sign of support for the apartheid policies of the South African government. Given the prevailing international academic boycotts at the time, any scholarly interest in this particular Italian diaspora may also have been curtailed at that time. The few existing texts from that time, such as those by Bini (1957) and Sani (1992), and a few that have been published since then, such as the work of Giuliani-Balestrini (1995), Macioti and Zaccai (2006), and Iacoponi (2013), focus on some important historical aspects related to the Italian community in South Africa but have not reflected specifically on the descendants of the original immigrant community and their sense of identity or their relationship with Italy. (This list of publications is not exhaustive.) The best-known research has been done on the experiences of the prisoners of war interned at Zonderwater in the small town of Cullinan during World War II (described in more detail in Chapter 4), by Annese (2010), Carlesso (2013), Sani (1992), and Somma (2007, 2010). These prisoners of war formed an important segment of the first-generation Italian immigrants in South Africa. Consequently, we decided to focus our research on the second- and third- generation Italians who are the descendants of this post–World War II diaspora. These two generations are also inextricably connected with the South African realities today, as white people of European descent living in South Africa.

Even though little academic attention has so far been dedicated to Italians in South Africa, the Italian community in this country is the most populous remaining Italian community on the entire African continent; a total of 35,874 were registered with the local Italian consular registry offices by 1 October 2022, and that excludes individuals of Italian descent who do not hold a dual passport. The Italian community is currently subject to the trend of young people leaving South Africa for what they perceive as better opportunities elsewhere, becoming part of the "brain drain" which has troubled South Africa since the early 1990s (Crush, 2000). Exact numbers and destinations of these out-migrants are difficult to extrapolate, but it does appear from anecdotal information from the local consulates that the majority of these emigrants have not "returned" to Italy but seem to have followed the common migration paths of other South Africans, choosing destinations such as Australia, New Zealand, and the United Kingdom. This choice reflects greater comfort with Anglophone countries, because of these migrants' familiarity with English (as an official language in South Africa) and the way of life in Anglophone countries. At the same time, as an equal and opposite phenomenon, South Africa is witnessing a new wave of Italian immigration, which is bringing into the country young professional Italians, usually highly qualified, who are part of the Italian "*fuga dei cervelli*" (brain drain) and who are able to find a job and get a visa despite the strict immigration laws in place in South Africa (Marchetti-Mercer & Virga, 2021).

This book deals with an under-researched and often ignored community, to contribute to an understanding of the complexity of Italian diasporas, especially in Africa. We concur with Gabaccia (2000) that it is impossible to speak of one Italian diaspora – it is more appropriate to speak of "diasporas", each reflective of the migration trends peculiar to a specific geographic destination, as well as to the unique socio-cultural characteristics of that destination country. We intersect with the colonial dimension to which the Italian migration in Africa is usually linked, but we also diverge from it by showing a different reality. In a sense, we wish to open up the African map of Italian migration both geographically – moving away from the Horn of Africa or North Africa – and historically, by exploring the Italian community in diaspora of today and not that of the past. This book also hopes to serve as an addition to the traditional research that has focused on migration to Africa as a result of the Italian colonial enterprise (see, for example, Morone, 2011; Ertola, 2019). A pertinent example is the case of those who migrated to Eritrea during the colonial period – some of them, and some of their descendants, subsequently moved to South Africa. The research described in this book is also unique in exploring a different migration trend, namely from the Global North to the

Global South, which is not reflective of Italian migration to Africa during the period of colonization up to World War II.

An overview of the research project

In the next chapter, we reflect in depth on the personal and professional paths which brought us together and the intersection at which the idea for the project was born. However, we first want to share with the reader the most salient aspects of the research project on which this book is based.

Our initial intention was to focus only on second-generation Italians living in South Africa. We defined a second-generation Italian immigrant as someone who had at least one parent who had immigrated to South Africa from Italy during or after World War II. Although there was Italian migration to South Africa prior to World War II (see Marchetti-Mercer & Virga, 2021), we saw the post-war period as the beginning of what we can today consider the Italian community in South Africa. However, when we put out the call for participants on various social media, as well as via our professional networks, we were contacted by a number of young people who self-identified as Italian and who were in fact third-generation Italians. This happened even though we made our inclusion criteria clear in our call for participants, stating that we were looking for participants whose parent(s) originally came from Italy. This unexpected interest in the research project and willingness to share their experiences was intriguing. We therefore decided to broaden the scope of our study to include the third generation. Based on what we found in our analysis of the data, it would probably have been quite difficult to differentiate clearly between second- and third-generation Italians, because the situation of some participants was in fact a mixture. For example, in some cases, participants had one grandparent born in Italy, and/or one parent on the other side of the family born in Italy. In terms of regional origins, we recruited participants with roots across the entire Italian peninsula, including Sicily and Sardinia. The oldest participant was 60 years old and the youngest was 18 years old. The majority had completed or were completing some post–high school or tertiary qualifications. All the participants who volunteered for the study had white parents and grandparents, which has strong implications for the findings of our study, as we show later in the book. However, we should not assume that all descendants of Italian immigrants are white; there are second- and third-generation Italians who come from a mixed-race background, such as poet Don (Donato Francisco) Mattera, whom we cited at the start of this chapter, and who had an Italian grandfather and a Xhosa grandmother.

From the outset, when we started conceptualizing this study, we chose ethnography as an appropriate methodology for our study. Its value lies in being able to apply multiple data collection methods to explore a single phenomenon. Given our own dual positions as researchers and also as members of the Italian community in South Africa, ethnography seemed a suitable approach.

Therefore, over and above our intention to interview participants, we also hoped to participate in cultural, social, and scientific events that included members of the Italian community and to include our observations among our findings. However, our initial plans were severely curtailed by the outbreak of the COVID-19 pandemic, which closed down all opportunities to participate in social activities from March 2020 up to the time when we started writing this book.

The pandemic has had a far-reaching and unexpected impact on how researchers across the world and in different disciplines carry out their work. While it has created many new opportunities and areas of focus such as tele-therapy (in the case of Psychology) and online research (see, for example, the work Nguyen et al., 2021), it has challenged the work of many other scholars who depended on physical participation and contact. Furthermore, the impact of the pandemic on our own professional and personal lives cannot be underestimated. We both teach at the same university, where almost overnight we had to adjust to emergency remote teaching, working in a very challenging socio-economic context with enormous financial disparities, feeding into a digital divide, as well as dealing with familial demands of our own, especially as mothers.

As part of our data collection process, we carried out semi-structured interviews with 30 participants. Two interviews had to be excluded from the final data analysis, however, as one of these participants was born in Italy and the other participant's parents emigrated to South Africa immediately after World War I. All the interviews except one were conducted in person. Most of the interviews took place in the Gauteng and Western Cape regions. Although there are prominent Italian communities in other provinces in South Africa, such as KwaZulu-Natal, the Eastern and the Northern Cape, we were limited by funding and lockdown constraints, which did not allow us to travel as widely as we would have liked; there was also little interest in participating among possible participants who were approached in some of these areas. It would arguably have been preferable to include a broader spectrum of participants, but the two geographic areas that we focused on are the ones where the majority of the Italian communities in South Africa are found. We also reached an acceptable level of saturation in the data. Consequently, we felt confident that the data collected were sufficiently representative of the phenomena we were trying to understand.

We used the thematic analysis approach developed by Braun and Clarke (2006) to analyse the data, as well as the reflexive journals that we kept during the data collection process. Suzuki et al. (2005) caution that being "insiders" may influence the interpretation of findings, so we took careful cognizance of our personal experiences and social location during the data analysis. Undeniably, and unapologetically, our own positionality in the project has played an important role in the entire process, and we believe that in the end this positionality proved to be a strength of the project as it unfolded.

Another challenge (or possible opportunity) was presented by the fact that we as researchers come from very distinct disciplines. This meant that the data we collected were potentially viewed through very different theoretical and professional lenses. We argue that this diversity added to the uniqueness of the project, as it allowed a much broader understanding of our participants' experiences, even if it meant that we needed to undergo a process of adjustment in order to find a common language. The data analysis therefore included a continuous process of discussion and dialogue as we went through the extensive coding process outlined by Braun and Clarke (2006). Throughout this process, discussions took place regarding the theoretical, methodological, and analytical choices that we made. In the analysis discussion, as decisions regarding the thematic analysis were being made, we included another colleague who is well-schooled in research methodology. Ultimately, we were able to reach a consensus on the identified themes. In the chapters where we discuss our specific findings, verbatim quotations from the participants are extensively used to show from where we drew our themes – analysis of such verbatim quotations enhances the accuracy and reliability of the research process (Morrison & James, 2009).

As with all research on human experiences, adherence to ethical principles was essential. We believe that the content explored in our interviews did not include what could be considered potentially upsetting material. We are also careful to protect the confidentiality of our participants' identities through the use of pseudonyms and have removed or adapted any information which may potentially identify them.

The identification of overarching themes was the aim of our thematic analysis, but we are cautious not to present the themes discussed in Chapters 5, 6, and 7 as fully representative of the Italian second and third generations in South Africa. We can only hope to describe the themes that emerged from the stories of the participants who shared their experiences with us.

About the book

The discussion of our findings relies heavily on the voices of our participants. Therefore, in this book we did not just present a summary of the interviews we held with them but we use their own words in the form of direct quotations in italics. We also provide a biographical note on each of the participants in Appendix A so that the reader can refer to this information to understand their family and historical backgrounds better while reading the relevant chapters.

The book is organized into three parts. In the first part, we reflect on a number of personal and theoretical issues, giving them both an equal voice, as we argue the important relationship between the personal and the professional in academic research. The second chapter (Meeting in the diaspora, researching the diaspora) provides an overview of our own personal and professional backgrounds. Our stories include information on our migration background, our positions in the Italian community, how we met in a professional context, and how the project came about. We also elaborate in depth on the process of writing the book in the framework of our interdisciplinary collaboration. In the third chapter (Theoretical context), we discuss the main theoretical concepts underlying the research, such as ethnic identity and *italianità*. We also provide an overview of theories on migrant assimilation, especially as they relate to the second and third generations. More recent theoretical views on transnationalism, mobility studies, and the diaspora are explored. This theoretical context will enhance readers' understanding of the context from which the study was born, and the main theories and discussions around our research topic. In Chapter 4 (Historical context of the Italian community), we briefly explore the history and legacy of Italian migration to South Africa during and after World War II, as well as developments in the Italian presence in South Africa in the context of the democratic post-apartheid dispensation after 1994. This historical context is discussed specifically to show how it relates to our participants and their families.

The second part of the book focuses on describing the main themes that emerged from the data analysis of the semi-structured interviews that we conducted with our participants. Chapter 5 (*"Our family does everything together"*: The importance of the family of origin) revolves around the role that the family of origin plays in transferring Italian culture and the Italian language to the second and third generations of Italians in South Africa. Our findings emphasize the function of family rituals related to religious/cultural norms, as well as the prominent role of grandparents in passing on a sense of cultural identity, and, closely interlinked with this, of Italian as a language. The cultural significance of food practices in these migrant families is also touched upon. Chapter 6 (*"I find it unique and I am proud to be Italian"*: The relationship with Italy and the larger Italian community in South Africa) explores our participants' sense of identity and connections with both Italy and South Africa. We investigate different popular cultural markers such as watching RAI International, and, more recently, RAI Italia, and interest in Italian sports and Italian music, versus limited interest in reading Italian books and newspapers, and a lack of involvement in the Italian political system, despite being allowed to vote for the Italian national elections where Italian citizenship is still in place. The chapter also explores participants' relationships with the larger Italian community, which, especially in the case of the third generation, seemed to translate into participation in youth associations. The last chapter of this second part, Chapter 7 (*"The point of going to Italy is the sense of belonging"*: The meaning of visits to Italy), investigates the role and the meaning that visits to Italy have for our participants. Visits often begin in childhood as a kind of cultural introduction to Italy and extended families and are carried on later in adulthood. These visits were experienced very positively by all the participants and were seen as a crucial tool to connect with their extended families. Visits also seemed to reinforce their sense of cultural identity and influence the relationship between participants and the Italian language.

The third part of the book aims to explain our findings from a more critical and analytical perspective. A prominent theme that emerged from our research is the strong sense of longing and nostalgia for Italy felt by members of the second and third generations of Italians living in South Africa. This longing seems to point to an imaginary idealizing perception of Italy and is closely linked to their search for a sense of belonging. We understand this construction of belonging against the current situation in South African society, which is still grappling with its own multicultural identity. In Chapter 8 (*"There is a lot of pain that I have inherited"*: Identity through nostalgia), we find the root of the nostalgia for Italy in the family of origin and therefore we interpret it as an inherited nostalgia. However, we also recognize that nostalgia is a tool to construct a place which people can identify with – a place called Italy, but which is, in fact, an imaginary space. Indeed, in instances where participants actually went to live in Italy, they often returned with a sense of great disillusionment. In Chapter 9 (*"I don't feel Italian there and I don't feel South African here"*: Finding belonging in an interliminal space), we take a step forward to acknowledge that the imaginary place constructed through nostalgia provides a sense of belonging for second- and third-generation Italians in South Africa. We read this in the context of the socio-political reality of the destination country today. We borrow the term "interliminality" from translation studies to provide a theoretical understanding of our participants' sometimes ambivalent experiences, which often manifest in contradictory beliefs and actions as they search for a place of belonging.

In the conclusion in Chapter 10, we summarize and reflect on the significance of the findings as they relate to the larger international body of work, and we suggest possible research going forward.

References

Annese, C. (2010). *I diavoli di Zonderwater. 1941–1947. La storia dei prigionieri italiani in Sudafrica che sopravvissero alla guerra grazie allo sport*. Sperling & Kupfer.

Baldassar, L. (1999). Marias and marriage: Ethnicity, gender and sexuality among Italo-Australian youth in Perth1. *Journal of Sociology, 35*(1), 1–22. https://doi.org /10.1177/144078339903500101

Baldassar, L. (2011). Italian migrants in Australia and their relationship to Italy: Return visits, transnational caregiving and the second generation. *Journal of Mediterranean Studies, 20*(2), Special Issue, "Of home, belonging and return: Transnational links of the Mediterranean-origin second generation" (edited by R. King & A. Christou), 255–282. https://www.muse.jhu.edu/article/672926

Bini, A. (1957). *Italiani in Sud Africa*. Scuole arti grafiche artigianelli.

Braun, V., & Clarke, V. (2006). Using thematic analysis in psychology. *Qualitative Research in Psychology, 3*(2), 77–101. https://doi.org/10.1191/1478088706qp063oa

Buranello, R. (2009). *Between fact and fiction: Italian immigration to South Africa* (pp. 23–44). Centro Altreitalie, Globus et Locus.

Carlesso, L. (2013). *Centomila prigionieri italiani in Sud Africa – Il Campo di Zonderwater*. Longo Editore.

Castles, S., & Davidson, A. (2020). *Citizenship and migration: Globalization and the politics of belonging*. Routledge.

Crush, J. (2000). *Losing our minds: Skills migration and the South African brain drain*. SAMP migration policy series No. 18. Southern African Migration Programme.

Ertola, E. (2019). *In terra d'Africa: Gli italiani che colonizzarono l'impero*. Gius Laterza & figli Spa.

Gabaccia, D. R. (2000). *Italy's many diasporas*. University of Washington Press.

Gans, H. J. (1982). *The urban villagers: Group and class in the life of Italian-Americans*. Free Press, Collier Macmillan.

Gilmartin, M. (2008). Migration, identity and belonging. *Geography Compass*, *2*(6), 1837–1852. https://doi.org/10.1111/j.1749-8198.2008.00162.x

Giuliani-Balestrino, M. C. (1995). *Gli Italiani nel Sud Africa*. Geocart Editors.

Haller, H. (2011). Varieties, use, and attitudes of Italian in the U.S.: The dynamics of an immigrant language through time. In T. Stehl (Ed.), *Sprachen in mobilisierten Kulturen: Aspekte der Migrationslinguistik* (Vol. 2, pp. 57–70). Universitätsverlag Potsdam.

Iacoponi, V. (2013). *Campi d'oro e strade di ferro. Il Sudafrica e l'immigrazione italiana tra Ottocento e Novecento*. XL Edizioni.

Macioti, M. I., & Zaccai, C. (2006). *Italiani in Sudafrica. Le trasformazioni culturali della migrazione*. Guerini scientifica.

Mangione, J., & Morreale, B. (1992). *La storia. Five centuries of Italian American experience*. HarperCollins.

Marchetti-Mercer, M. C., & Virga, A. (2021). The Italian diaspora in South Africa: Origins and identity. *Italian Studies*. https://doi.org/10.1080/00751634.2021.1923174

Marino, S. (2019). Ethnic identity and race: The "double absence" and its legacy across generations among Australians of Southern Italian origin. Operationalizing institutional positionality. *Ethnic and Racial Studies*, *42*(5), 707–725. https://doi.org/10.1080/01419870.2018.1451649

Marino, S. (2020). An intergenerational conceptualisation of Italian-Australian ethnic identity through Bourdieu and Heidegger. *Social Identities*, *26*(1), 3–15. https://doi.org/10.1080/13504630.2019.1664286

Marino, S. (2021). Thrown into the world: The shift between pavlova and pasta in the ethnic identity of Australians originating from Italy. *Journal of Sociology*, *57*(2), 231–248. https://doi.org/10.1177/1440783319888283

Mattera, D. (2009). *Memory is the weapon*. African Perspectives Publications.

Milanese, A. (2002). *Italians in South Africa: Challenges in the representation of an Italian identity* [Master's thesis, University of Cape Town]. https://open.uct.ac.za/handle/11427/7953

Morone, A. M. (2011). Italiani d'africa, africani d'Italia: Da coloni a profughi. *Altreitalie*, *42*, 20–35.

Morrison, M., & James, S. (2009). Portuguese immigrant families: The impact of acculturation. *Family Process*, *48*(1), 151–166. https://doi.org/10.1111/j.1545-5300.2009.01273.x

Nguyen, H. T., Baldassar, L., Wilding, R., & Krzyzowski, L. (2021). Researching older Vietnam-born migrants at a distance: The role of digital kinning. In H. Kara & S. M. Khoo (Eds.), *Qualitative and digital research in times of crisis: Methods, reflexivity, and ethics* (pp. 172–190). Policy Press.

Piccoli, G. (2014). *Italian immigration in the United States* [Doctoral dissertation, Duquesne University]. https://dsc.duq.edu/etd/1044

Sala, E. (2017). *The Italian-ness is in the family: A critical evaluation of the role of family in constructions of ethnicity and connections to homeland among two cohorts of second generation Italian-Australians* [Doctoral thesis, University of Western Australia]. https://api.research-repository.uwa.edu.au/ws/portalfiles/portal /20507794/THESIS_DOCTOR_OF_PHILOSOPHY_SALA_Emanuela_2017.pdf

Sala, E., & Baldassar, L. (2017a). "I don't do much in the community as an Italian, but in my family I do": A critique of symbolic ethnicity through a longitudinal study of second-generation Italian Australians. *Journal of Anthropological Research*, *73*(4), 557–583. https://doi.org/10.1086/694683

Sala, E., & Baldassar, L. (2017b). Leaving family to return to family: Roots migration among second-generation Italian-Australians. *Ethos*, *45*(3), 386–408. https://doi .org/10.1111/etho.12173

Sani, G. (1992). *History of the Italians in South Africa 1489–1989*. Zonderwater Block.

Skrbiš, Z. (2008). Transnational families: Theorising migration, emotions and belonging. *Journal of Intercultural Studies*, *29*(3), 231–246. https://doi.org/10.1080 /07256860802169188

Skrbiš, Z., Baldassar, L., & Poynting, S. (2007). Introduction – Negotiating belonging: Migration and generations. *Journal of Intercultural Studies*, *28*(3), 261–269. https:// doi.org/10.1080/07256860701429691

Somma, D. (2010). Music as discipline, solidarity and nostalgia in the Zonderwater prisoner of war camp of South Africa. *SAMUS: South African Music Studies*, *30*(1), 71–85. https://hdl.handle.net/10520/EJC133297

Somma, D. A. (2007). *Mythologising music: Identity and culture in the Italian prisoner of war camps of South Africa* [Doctoral dissertation, University of the Witwatersrand]. https://issuu.com/zonderwater/docs/tesi_di_donato_andrew _somma_su_zonderwater

Suzuki, L. A., Ahluwalia, M. K., Mattis, J. S., & Quizon, C. A. (2005). Ethnography in counseling psychology research: Possibilities for application. *Journal of Counseling Psychology*, *52*(2), 206–214. https://doi.org/10.1037/0022-0167.52.2.206

Wessendorf, S. (2007). "Roots migrants": Transnationalism and "return" among second-generation Italians in Switzerland. *Journal of Ethnic and Migration Studies*, *33*(7), 1083–1102. https://doi.org/10.1080/13691830701541614

Wessendorf, S. (2008). *Negotiating Italianità: Ethnicity and peer-group formation among transnational second-generation Italians in Switzerland*. University of Sussex, Sussex Centre of Migration Research.

Wessendorf, S. (2010). Local attachments and transnational everyday lives: Second-generation Italians in Switzerland. *Global Networks*, *10*(3), 365–382. https://doi.org/10.1111/j.1471-0374.2010.00293.x

Wessendorf, S. (2016). *Second-generation transnationalism and roots migration: Cross-border lives*. Routledge.

2 Meeting in the diaspora, researching the diaspora

Positioning ourselves

All academic research starts with us and within us. Whether we are conscious of it or not, there is always a reason for our choosing to do research on one particular topic rather than on another. More often than we realize, that reason has more to do with ourselves than with academic questions. Undoubtedly, questions raised by academe often determine the course of our research and shape it. Nevertheless, the initial impetus and our motivation do not rest merely on academic enquiry. Hence, we are compelled to talk about ourselves in this chapter before discussing the theoretical basis of our research.

There are many sound academic reasons for writing this book, including the lacunae already mentioned in Chapter 1, and these add to why we believe this book is unique in its genre. But there are also personal stories and motivations that spurred us to embark on this journey. As Black et al. (2019) aptly say,

> [i]t is impossible to separate the personal from the professional, but we recognize that a pressure exists; we feel this pressure – detaching from 'self' is the 'professional' thing to do isn't it? Our workplace structures seem to communicate that such separation is appropriate.
>
> (p. 532)

We strongly believe that who we are has a lot to do with what we write, how we write, and what we see in our scientific investigations. In Western and Westernized universities, there is a long tradition of academic research that claims to be based on the principle of objectivity, in which the personal position of the researcher should not influence, and should not have anything to do with, academic enquiry and writing. This is, however, a very questionable tradition, which derives from a patriarchal hegemonic position which was fully adopted by neoliberal institutions such as universities around the world. The self, made up of specific stories and bodies, has been erased by this tradition, and diversity is not acknowledged. All who want to be scholars have been expected to comply with a specific way of writing, and needed to erase themselves in this process. Instead, we make the claim that it is especially in the

DOI: 10.4324/9781003266884-2

process of writing that our specific beings develop and emerge. Not recognizing this would mean suppressing our identities to comply with a questionable hegemonic tradition. We are convinced of the need to oppose this hegemony and let our stories and our voices emerge in order to honour also the voices of our participants.

We tell our personal stories to be transparent about and accountable for the way in which our stories relate to the research presented in this book. By doing so, we position ourselves as the authors of this book – as two female academics writing from the Global South and coming from and with a history of migration. We therefore embrace a position similar to Black et al.'s (2019):

> This deliberate breaking open of the hegemonic spaces of the academy is a methodology that also opens spaces for our/women's visibility, voice and agency; spaces to acknowledge our embodied dimensions in order to emancipate our bodies from their erasure of these hegemonic spaces; to locate spaces beyond measurement, impact, evidence and all the violent organisational enterprises the hegemonic spaces of the academy produce.
>
> (pp. 532–533)

Both of us are scholars of Italian origin. We both live in Johannesburg, South Africa. We both work at the same university, the University of the Witwatersrand, in the Faculty of Humanities, although we work in two different academic fields, namely Psychology and Italian Studies. We have different experiences of migration; we belong to different generations. However, both of us, at different moments in our lives, began to think about our respective conditions as migrants, and we met at the juncture of these experiences and reflections. We therefore briefly tell our personal stories and how they intersected, because it is at this meeting point that the idea for the project described in this book was born. We also reflect on the process of writing this book, which created something new, not only in the form of words written on paper but also in our relationship with our own migrant identities, our relationship with each other, and with our individual theoretical positions.

Our position, both in geographical space and in time, has important implications for the content of the book; our personal geographies and temporal positions became epistemological points from which we look at our object of investigation. This book would not have been the same if both of us were not Italian-born female immigrants living in South Africa. With this in mind, let us now introduce ourselves and explain how we became members of the Italian diaspora in South Africa.

Maria's story

When I was 11 years old, my parents decided to move from Italy to South Africa. At that stage of my life, I really had no idea what consequences this event would have for my future. I clearly remember being somewhat excited at the prospect of this new adventure. I was anxious about the fact that I could not speak English and intuitively understood that what I had learnt in primary school in Milan would be insufficient to survive in the new country where I would live. I was sad about leaving my friends behind, as we were about to enter middle school, something to which I had really looked forward. I was heartbroken at the prospect of leaving my cats and dogs behind.

I vaguely understood that my parents had made the decision to leave Italy because they wanted to give me a better future, by leaving a country that in the 1970s was racked by political violence and terrorism. Like many parents throughout history, they decided to leave their country of birth "for the sake of their children". This decision was to set my life onto an unknown, and very different, course than would have been the case if I had stayed in Milan and entered the Europa Scuola Media in September 1975. Instead, I found myself starting the last term of what was then the Standard 5 class of Clarendon Primary School for girls in East London. These schools were worlds apart, not only geographically but also culturally and psychologically. Within a week, I moved from being the top student in my class with friends and a very secure place in my social circle to being the odd girl out, an awkward pre-teen who did not understand a word that was being spoken around her, a girl who elicited mild interest from her peers, until they realized that communication was impossible, a girl with no friends and no place in the world.

Was it all so hard? Of course not. People were generally welcoming, and the country was so very beautiful. We settled in the Eastern Cape region of South Africa, a place with unparalleled natural beauty. Slowly but surely, I began to understand what was being said; despite retaining an accent, which I have never quite managed to let go of, and through sheer persistence I learnt English. I even started learning to speak Afrikaans, and strangely, found that I had an aptitude for this very foreign-sounding language with its guttural sounds so alien to the Italian ear. I wanted to "belong", whatever that meant in the South Africa of the 1970s. I soon let go of most things Italian, except for the language, which we continued to speak at home, something I am very grateful for today. I did not want to stand out any more than my funny-sounding surname unavoidably already caused me to do.

My parents became very involved in the Italian community living in the Eastern Cape, so many of our closest friends were from this group. Some friends we had in Milan also moved to South Africa, and one family even brought with them one of our original "Italian" dogs, which they had adopted when we left Italy. My mother became the Italian honorary consul for what was then called the Border region and held that position for more than 30 years. During that time, she worked tirelessly to bring together the Italian community in that area and to promote Italy's image in the Eastern Cape. I have very fond memories of Italian National days and Christmas parties. The most memorable of all was the procession my mother organized through the main streets of East London when Italy won the World Cup in 1982. The whole Italian community drove their cars through town, hooting and waving the Italian national flag.

The first time I returned to Italy after our emigration was six years later, after I had already written my final high school exams. I did not really want to be in Italy and felt little connection with the land of my birth. It was 11 years later that I next returned to Italy, after I had completed my master's degree in Clinical Psychology, and I returned to work towards a doctorate at the Milan School of Family Therapy. Ironically, it was because of my interest in family therapy that I returned to Italy. During my MA in Clinical Psychology studies, I discovered that some of the most important schools of family therapy had been established in Italy during the 1970s. The one I was most fascinated with was right in the centre of Milan. It was run by an Italian psychiatrist-turned-family-therapist, Mara Selvini Palazzoli. I spent two weeks at the Centre for the Study of the Family in Milan in the summer of 1991, and the course of my life, both professionally and personally, began to change. I discovered a professional field that really appealed to me and with which I could identify, and I fell in love with Italy again.

Coming back to South Africa after that visit was very difficult. I found myself having to engage in the constant struggle that characterizes most emigrants' lives – one of having to move continually between two worlds, always longing for one or the other, inhabiting the world of liminality.

Shortly thereafter, another story of emigration was to touch my life, namely the peregrinations of my future husband. When I met Chris, I encountered another story of migration to foreign climes. He came from Northern Ireland, had been educated at a university in England, and then worked in the United States for 11 years, where he was to become a naturalized citizen. Subsequently, while pursuing further postgraduate studies in Britain, he was headhunted by the Centre for Scientific and Industrial Research (CSIR) in South Africa, and he arrived in South Africa in 1990, just after the unbanning of the African National Congress (ANC). The Italian Catholic girl from Milan, then lecturing psychology at an Afrikaans-speaking university, collided with a globetrotting Irish Protestant with a distinct American accent. This lucky intersection of two independent paths was to weave a rich tapestry of belief systems and ideologies that continues to find unique expression in the lives of our two children, Connor and Francesca, for whom South Africa became the land of their birth.

In the years that followed our starting a family, we found ourselves losing many friends and colleagues who emigrated to other parts of the world. There were times that my husband and I also considered leaving the country, but in the end, we always decided to stay. Perhaps, between the two of us, we had already moved plenty of times during our lifetimes.

After a family therapy training course in Rome in 2004, for which I spent a long period in Italy, I felt compelled to try to understand my own need to "belong" and, consequently, how to define what I considered to be "home". These issues of belonging and home are part and parcel of every migrant's experience. I began researching the stories of South African families whose adult children were leaving or had left the country. I read and wrote extensively on the process of migration and the impact of emigration on families, especially those who stayed behind, who had to cope with the loss of children, grandchildren, and other loved ones. It was during this time of professional and personal growth that my mother emailed me a piece from a local Italian newspaper written by an Italian academic working at the same university as I was. I had never met her, as we work in different departments, and yet I found her words deeply moving. I decided to email her and invite her for a cup of coffee.

Anita's story

I left Italy when I was 25. In my mind, I was not leaving forever. I was going to the United States to further my studies, open to what life held in store for me. But there was something of which I was sure: I would always come back to Italy as much as I could. Before leaving, one of my cousins told me that with time I would come back less and less, until a time would come in which I would not come back at all. "Not me," I thought.

At that time, I did not consider myself a migrant. I was just a young person who was moving away to pursue her studies. Once I was in the States, I used to leave for Italy the day after the semester was over and go back to the States the day before the semester began. Every time. I remember that a few years in, I encountered for the first time the books of the so-called Italian "migrant writers", such as Igiaba Scego and Gabriella Ghermandi. Amongst other issues, they reflected on their identity, what it meant for them to be Italian, what it meant for them to be considered foreigners by other Italians, what it meant for them to speak and write in Italian. At that time, I could not really understand why they were making such a big deal out of these issues. Why was it so important for them to reflect on their identity? "I am an Italian living in the States, that is it," I remember thinking. Not a big deal. Nothing to really care about so much and about which to lose sleep at night.

A few years later, I felt that Connecticut, where I was living at that time, had given me all it had to offer. It was as if the initial energy was fading away. It was time to move. I was single, I could go wherever I wanted, and there were no limits to my imagination. For some reason, even before moving to the United States, I had always thought that one day I would like to live in South Africa. I started looking for a job before finishing my PhD thesis, and someone told me about a position at a university in South Africa. I immediately applied and they short-listed me, offering me a Skype interview. I panicked a little bit – it is one thing to dream about going somewhere else, another actually to do it. During my job interview – for the occasion I moved my table-desk so that a bookshelf could feature in the background – I thought that I would have liked to be on the other side of the screen. One month later, they offered me the possibility to be on that other side and they gave me five days to decide whether to accept the job offer. I consulted my parents and they were against the idea – and anyway, who goes from the United States to South Africa for a job? My colleagues told me that South Africa is a dangerous place – which was confirmed by any Google search that I attempted; I clearly remember someone describing an incident in which a gun was pointed at him. The warnings were loud and clear: "Do not go to South Africa." There was also a very practical difficulty: I was not leaving my parents' home. In the few years I had spent in the United States, I had accumulated a certain number of belongings. Some I could have shipped to South Africa, but others, such as my car and my furniture, would have to be sold or given away; I could not leave anything behind with the idea of going back and getting it at a later stage. This was a one-way ticket. (Now I realize that all of this meant that I did not have roots in the United States – but at that time I was just focusing on the practical aspects, because I still had not internalized the idea that I was a migrant.) The odds were clearly against my second migration. But I closed my eyes, and I decided to go. There was a specific moment in which this happened – a sudden moment in which I felt that it was right to go. I wonder what my life would have been now if that moment had not happened.

I did not know anyone in South Africa prior to my arrival, nor had I ever been there. I knew little more than a bit about Mandela and the soccer World Cup of 2010. I watched a few movies before leaving, and that was the sum total of my knowledge of South Africa. I moved in February 2013, and I spent the Christmas before, packing my stuff with the help of my parents in the United States. That was the first Christmas I spent away from Italy, but at least I was still with my parents. My cousin's prediction was slowly coming true, but I ignored the signs.

When I arrived in South Africa, I was alone. I landed at a university where there were thousands and thousands of people, quickly realizing that when there are many people you are even more isolated. I had to finish my PhD thesis under quite adverse conditions and battled against a long depression. It took me months to settle in and years to build a social network. Little by little, I started integrating with the Italian community in Johannesburg on one hand, and with local South Africans on the other. My English improved dramatically, especially when I started dating South African people, but my Italian was slowly leaving me. Sometimes I caught myself searching for a word while I was speaking Italian, and this happened increasingly. When I went back to Italy, I began to realize that the language spoken there was a little bit different from the Italian I remembered and the one I was used to speaking in South Africa. I was going from the extreme of an academic and literary vocabulary to an impoverished Italian, in which many of the words used were English. Neither of these two languages reflected what was spoken in Italy at the time.

Summers in South Africa are beautiful, and for someone who always preferred warm weather, it seemed a pity to go back to Italy over Christmas. I started skipping a few Christmas visits back to Italy. With my work and my various commitments in South Africa, I also started shortening my visits. One day my father called me to convey the news that one of my aunts had passed away unexpectedly. During the following days I found it difficult to understand the meaning of this. Something was happening in Italy while I was not there. The next time I would be there, I would find something different that would not match the image that I held in my mind when I left, and that I carried with me all the time. The first time that I visited my widowed uncle, even though I knew my aunt was no longer there, I still had the impression that at any time she would appear from the other room. But this never happened. I was seeing the shadows of my broken soul. Because something inside me was indeed broken.

I became aware that Italy was becoming a distant reality to me, both in space and in time. I was also becoming a distant entity from Italy. I realized I was now a migrant; that on the day when I left Italy to go to study in Connecticut, I had already become a migrant. The process of recognition was slower than the process of leaving. I also began to understand that there was a pain in me which I had never experienced before. I started wondering who I was, what it meant for me to be Italian, and what my sense of belonging was. One day, for the first time, I wrote something about it. At that point – again – I did not completely grasp what I was doing. I thought I was just writing something about what I was feeling. Instead, another process was set in motion. Shortly after, I received an email from an Italian colleague of mine, a full professor, whom I knew only by name. She had read the piece I had written, and she wanted to meet me over coffee.

The meeting point

Maria: Anita accepted my invitation for a coffee. We met at the university's art gallery's coffee shop and started sharing our stories and reflections on the migrant experience and our work. We did not know it yet, but this was to be the beginning of our collaboration, and most importantly, the beginning of our friendship. Anita was also my first real Italian friend, as in the 40 odd years I had been in South Africa, I had mostly developed social connections with local South Africans. Throughout my adult life I had struggled with the same issues that many of our participants shared during this research process, namely the dual and often conflicting sense of identity and need to "belong" somewhere. As part of my other research on transnational families, I encountered the work of Loretta Baldassar, who has written extensively on the experiences of second-generation Italians living in Australia. I was drawn to her work, especially as it related to younger generation migrants' visits back to Italy. The stories of Baldassar's participants spoke to my own experience, and to the wonderful and emotionally intense visits I experienced as an adult to the country, the land, I had left as a child. I was aware that research related to Italians living in South Africa was primarily focused on their historical presence. Nothing I had read gave me a sense of the actual experiences and identity of this community. I started talking to Anita about a possible research project and how we could bring our different professional backgrounds together.

Anita: I distinctly remember that meeting at the coffee shop of the Wits art gallery. I was surprised to receive an email about the piece I had written about my migrant experience. Somehow, Maria understood that sharing this experience might also indicate an inclination to undertake research on this topic. I, on the other hand, had never thought about it. The idea of working together, investigating the sense of identity of Italians in South Africa, was an intriguing one. I had read something about the history of Italians in South Africa, but I had never encountered anything beyond this historical descrip-tion. Furthermore, I had never before conducted research involving human beings in the flesh. I had only been concerned with those that materialize in the pages of a book or those two-dimensional others on a screen. It prom-ised to be an exciting new intellectual adventure. I would make available my (albeit limited) knowledge of the Italian community of Johannesburg and my background in critical theories; Maria would use her experience as a clinical psychologist with a specific interest in family therapy.

Maria and Anita's "story" – writing the book

The process of data collection and analysis in qualitative research often receives detailed attention in the methodology section of any project, but two aspects of our research stand out for us: what it means to work in an interdis-ciplinary manner, and how that reveals itself in the process of writing up one's research – in our case, in the writing up of this book.

One of the strengths of this work is that we come from very different disci-plinary backgrounds: Psychology and Family Therapy *vs.* Italian Studies and Literature. When we first conceptualized the project, we compartmentalized the work into different and quite separate components, according to our own professional training, theoretical strengths, and academic interests. However, research is never quite so clear-cut, and we soon discovered that compartmen-talization is not really the goal of interdisciplinary research. This became very clear at two specific points of the research project.

The first was the data analysis, when we immersed ourselves in the mate-rial, and we went through the interviews and discussed our observations and perceptions, often bringing quite different points of view to the table before we eventually agreed on the themes. The second and perhaps most telling aspect was the process of writing the book. We had decided at the planning stage that each of us would take responsibility for writing certain chapters. And indeed, the first writing-up of some draft material took this format. However, we seemed to get stuck and the work did not progress. We then decided that perhaps we should sit together on Sundays at Anita's house and start writing our "different" pieces together as a way to motivate each other. We sat at her dining room table while Anita's young daughter watched cartoons on TV and played outside in the garden with her friends. We drank coffee and ate pizza, and we started writing. Actually, we started writing and *talking*. We began sharing our thoughts, reading pieces to each other, commenting on what we thought we were trying to say. We did this in a mixture of Italian and English (a bit like many of our participants). While Maria's spoken Italian is still reasonably good and she can read and understand Italian fully, her written Italian is not equally good. She would also struggle at times to speak "academic" Italian. Anita lectures Italian and some of her conceptualizations were developed in Italian, but at times she struggled to translate those into academic English. Therefore, we started helping each other out and we would often explain what we were trying to say to each other in a different language. When Anita would get stuck writing something in English, Maria often would say: "Explain to me in Italian what you want to say" and then we would try to "translate" it into an English equivalent. Sometimes Maria could not explain in proper academic Italian what her thinking was behind a certain argument, and Anita in her turn would help her with the proper academic language. We therefore started "translating" and "helping" each other, not only with unfamiliar language but also with unfamiliar concepts. The process of writing together and trying to achieve a real sense of interdisciplinarity began.

We met many more times after that, not only at Anita's house, but also at each other's offices on campus, and at coffee shops. We organized a "writing retreat" at a hotel near Wits University where we spent three full days writing. Not only did we continue our own process of writing and "translating", but we also started speaking about our own experiences of migration, our life stories, and how we had experienced the situations described by our participants. Eventually, we looked at chapters together, discussed changes, and wrote those together in a way that in the end made it difficult to see who had written what. In the final analysis it will also be difficult to recognize in the writing where the different disciplines of the authors lie. This has hopefully resulted in an authentic example of interdisciplinarity, where the final product is not arrived at by looking at the same data from different and distinct theoretical lenses but by creating something new together.

Some may criticize this approach and question its academic rigour. However, we believe that as two women in academia where interdisciplinarity is often encouraged but in practice rarely achieved, our methodology can serve as an example of how to work together in a truly respectful way: no single discipline is better than another; a researcher's seniority in the academic hierarchy does not necessarily impart "special" knowledge. The outcome is a creation of something different. This was, in a way, a process of translating our own migratory experiences into an academic work. We come back to the process of translation in Chapter 8 and to how, in the process of translating, a new space may be inhabited.

References

Black, A. L., Crimmins, G., & Henderson, L. (2019). Positioning ourselves in our academic lives: Exploring personal/professional identities, voice and agency. *Discourse: Studies in the Cultural Politics of Education, 40*(4), 530–544. https://doi .org/10.1080/01596306.2017.1398135

3 Theoretical context

Introduction

Migration is a widespread phenomenon which has changed in form and expression in recent decades. Italy, which used to be a country of emigration only, has now also become a destination for immigration, while some members of its population still continue to migrate elsewhere. As migratory fluxes and mobilities have increasingly become a characteristic of our globalized world, questions on how immigrants adapt to their destination country, how the destination country manages the influx of people from other parts of the world, and, significant for our study, how the children and grandchildren of immigrants live out their complex identities, have become more relevant.

In this chapter, we map out the theoretical terrain that guided our understanding and interpretation of the data collected. Not all concepts were explicitly used in our interpretation of the data; nevertheless, they provided the backdrop against which we discuss our participants' experiences in the second part of the book. Therefore, what we describe in this chapter is not an exhaustive overview of all the research that may be relevant to all second- and third-generation immigrants' experiences. We selected concepts and theories that come from various disciplines, such as psychology, sociology, anthropology, geography and migration studies; however, in our discussion we do not differentiate between disciplines or apply boundaries. Instead, we discuss these constructs from a broad perspective.

A definition of second- and third-generation immigrants

There is no consensus in the literature regarding how to define second- and third-generation immigrants. While we acknowledge that at some point every immigrant in the destination country is also an emigrant from the country of origin, we choose to refer to immigrants, since our study focuses on the experiences of those in the destination country. The second generation are usually regarded as the children of one or both original migrants. The third generation is then those with at least one grandparent from the country of origin. Levitt and Waters (2002) also refer to the "1.5" generation, which refers to those who migrated with their parents as children, and attended school and grew up

DOI: 10.4324/9781003266884-3

in the country of destination. King and Christou (2010) question whether it is really important to define what constitutes a second generation; they argue that while this may be relevant in terms of population statistics, it may not always qualitatively reflect the experience of individual people. Furthermore, one also encounters "mixed marriages" where only one parent or grandparent was an immigrant (Christou & King, 2010). For the purposes of our research, we included participants who were born in South Africa, where at least one parent/grandparent was born in Italy and where the original migrant(s) came to South Africa during or after World War II.

Ethnic identity

When it comes to defining ethnic identity, there are contrasting theoretical perspectives; some reflect essentialist perspectives, and others adopt a postmodern approach (Sala, 2017). The essentialist perspective emphasizes a well-defined sense of self and identity, one which is bounded and unique against a social and natural background, for example, the work of Geertz (1979). By contrast, social constructionism stresses the role played by social structures and processes in the formation of self and identity, and it explores the historical and ideological practices that inform these structures and processes, as exemplified in the work of Foucault (1988a, 1988b). From this perspective, the self is a more fluid concept, strongly influenced by a person's social contexts and experiences (Marchetti-Mercer, 2006).

Sala (2017), drawing on the work of Raffaetà et al. (2016), argues that "ethnicity ... can be conceptualised, understood and performed as simultaneously essentialist and constructivist, concurrently static and flexible" (p. 42), adding that a "particular focus on family does not exclude other important domains such as the influence of history or of the state" (p. 42). This emphasis on an interplay between essentialist/core values, as well as more dynamic and socially constructed values, including a focus on the important role of the family in conjunction with the larger social reality, results in a hybrid perspective – what Sala (2017) calls a contrapuntal perspective on ethnic identity. This suggests an interaction between continuity and change. In respect of migrant experiences, this may translate into a situation where "ethnicity is constructed in first generations and then reproduced and reconstructed in second generations" (Sala, 2017, p. 31). Consequently, the role of the family of origin and the larger social context of the destination country in which immigrant families find themselves are both significant.

This crucial role of the family of origin and larger community is also reflected in the work of McGoldrick et al. (2005), who emphasize the transgenerational transmission of ethnicity:

> the concept of a group's 'peoplehood' refers to a group's commonality of ancestry and history, through which people have evolved shared values and customs over the centuries. Based on a combination of race, religion,

and cultural history, ethnicity is retained, whether or not members realize their commonalities with one another. Its values are transmitted over generations by the family and reinforced by the surrounding community. It is a powerful influence in determining identity.

(p. 6)

Family therapists such as Andolfi (2005, 2016), Di Nicola (1997), Falicov (2005, 2007, 2011), and McGoldrick et al. (2005) have highlighted the significant role that the family of origin plays in the development of a cultural identity in younger migrant generations, and have examined the nature of their relationship with their forebears' country of origin.

Families of origin are a crucial point of reference from which we first learn what it means to "belong", and they create a sense of "home". The family in which we grow up is the first site for the development of our sense of personal and cultural identity (Marchetti-Mercer, 2006). In the case of second and third generations, the relationship and attachment with the country of origin of immigrants' forebears is not personal but is rather mediated through the relationship to family elders and ancestors and is often based on their memories and imagination (Falicov, 2007).

As indicated above, Sala (2017) also highlights the role of the family of origin in the formation of ethnicity, using Epstein's (1978) concept of "intimate culture", which refers to the subtle expressions of ethnic behaviours that are revealed in the family and home (Sala, 2017, p. 44). This is closely linked to what Reay (1998) describes as the "familial habitus", which refers to a "deeply ingrained system of perspectives, experiences and predispositions family members share" (p. 527). He bases his argument on Bourdieu's construct of a habitus as "the learned set of preferences or dispositions by which a person orients to the social world. It is a system of durable, transposable, cognitive 'schemata or structures of perception, conception and action'" (Bourdieu, 2002, p. 27). Ethnicity can also become a "boundary", with both symbolic and social aspects, which provides a distinction that individuals use to make and shape their actions and mental orientations towards other people (Alba, 2005). The idea of boundaries is also closely linked to self-identification, which relates to the way in which people define themselves in terms of the groups they feel they belong to.

Based on this brief overview of ethnic identity, we concur with Marino (2020), who sees ethnic identity as "both broad and particular, [...] a multifaceted subject that is difficult to unpack, since it relates to both an individual's collective social fields and his or her personal ones" (p. 5).

Italianità

Closely linked to the concept of ethnic identity and specifically relevant to our work is the construct of *italianità*. We are very aware that this is not an easily definable concept. *Italianità*, translated into English as Italian-ness, is a culturally and historically constructed and changeable concept, fluid and ambiguous by nature. Using the term without definition for a specific argument poses the risk of essentialism, as it can be used to create the myth of an innate characteristic which defines in a transcendental manner who is Italian and what the Italian "nature" and culture entail.

In the social sciences, scholars have used the term in different ways. Wessendorf (2016) defines *italianità* as a "set of values, practices and beliefs an individual associates with 'being' and 'doing' Italian" (p. 20). Both Sala (2017) and Wessendorf (2016) see *italianità* "as a way of creating a symbolic boundary between their group and the majority society" (Wessendorf, 2016, p. 75), a view which resonates with Alba's (2005) view on the boundaried nature of ethnicity. Sala (2017), in her research on second-generation Australians, found that her participants tended rather to use the term Italian-ness, so she argues that *italianità* tends to be primarily an academic term. Her view coincides with that of Baldassar and Pesman (2005) and Wessendorf (2016).

We contend that the understanding of the concept that is adopted depends on both historical and contingent factors: although the construct is historically determined, it also changes according to the contingency of the moment in time and in space. It is influenced by social and political events in Italy, but, for Italians living abroad, also by social and political events in the destination country. Viola and Verheul (2019), for example, comparing the construction of Italian ethnicity in newspapers in the United States and Italy between 1867 and 1920, discovered that *italianità* assumed a different meaning in these two contexts: in the United States it was constructed in such a way as to promote assimilation in the destination country, but in Italy it was constructed in such a way as to maintain political stability emphasizing national unity. A similar conclusion was reached by Pierno (2011), who investigated the renegotiation of *italianità* in Massachusetts through the use of the Italian language in a local Italian newspaper between the end of the 19th century and the beginning of the 20th century, compared to coeval Italian newspapers. Abroad, the sense of *italianità* needed to be renegotiated according to the local situation. Choate (2012) argues that

> [f]or Italy in the twenty-first century, ethnicity is defined by an Italian and European Union passport, with overt economic, cultural, and transnational ties. Legally, *Italianità* was defined by blood inheritance; more broadly, by a rich inheritance of culture, language, and tradition, untrammeled by state regulation and political boundaries.
>
> (p. 63)

Italianità has certainly been a key concept used to define both Italians living in Italy and Italians living abroad. From this perspective, we can argue that *italianità* is also a transnational concept, and, although it sets the boundaries of who is Italian and who is not, these boundaries go beyond physical and national ones. Indeed, *italianità* is not a sense that one can experience only in Italy; quite the contrary, as Parati and Tamburri (2011) point out: "Creating an 'Italy' outside of Italy is the goal of practices of *Italianità*" (p. 4). If the sense of *italianità* changes according to time and space, there is more than one way of experiencing it. Furthermore, even if it is a trait description ideally meant to unify people, *italianità* may also change according to one's personal experience, history, and way of thinking. Therefore, we use the term *italianità* to describe cultural constructions of anything connected to Italy, its people, and the Italian language, in the context of present South African society.

Arriving in a new country – first-generation migrants

Research has examined the preferred psychological and social outcomes of migration. Traditional models of migration regarded assimilation into the destination culture as an indication of successful migration (see, for example, relevant discussions in the work of Alba & Nee, 1997; Gordon, 1961). Verhaeghe et al. (2020) argue that classical assimilation theory believed that migrants' identification with the majority group would strengthen over time, overtaking their identification with the culture of origin. The concept of assimilation is also connected to the concept of the "melting pot" (Hirschman, 1983) that has often been used to describe the experiences of immigrants in American society. Consequently, maintaining strong cultural connections to one's country of origin was seen as a potential impediment to a successful migratory outcome. Moreover, assimilation was expected to be challenging for first-generation immigrants, but it was expected of second- and third-generation immigrants, especially if assimilation was likely to enhance social and economic success in the destination country.

The emphasis on the value of assimilation into the destination country has met with some criticism. For example, Di Nicola (1997) and Falicov (1995) regard assimilation more as an ideological outcome and requirement than as necessarily the most favourable psychological outcome for those concerned. Falicov (1995) criticizes the demand for assimilation imposed on immigrants, which reflects a certain ideology rather than an empirical inevitability. Such a demand suggests that the destination country is unable to tolerate difference (Marchetti-Mercer, 2017).

Berry (1992, 1997, 2001, 2005) has formulated a comprehensive model to describe the different acculturation strategies available to migrant populations, namely assimilation, integration, separation, and marginalization. The process of acculturation is described as

> the dual process of cultural and psychological change that takes place as a result of contact between two or more cultural groups and their individual members. At the group level, it involves changes in social

structures and institutions and in cultural practices. At the individual level, it involves changes in a person's behavioural repertoire.

(Berry, 2005, pp. 698–699)

Assimilation thus occurs when immigrants do not maintain their original cultural affiliation and are eventually absorbed into the culture of the destination country. Integration occurs when immigrants maintain their original cultural affiliation to some extent, but simultaneously participate in, and become part of the new culture. By contrast, separation is experienced by those who remain loyal to their own culture and do not interact with the new culture. Those immigrants who reject both cultures may eventually experience marginalization (Klingenberg et al., 2021). It is important to note that these adaptation strategies do not depend only on the immigrants themselves, but also on society in the destination country, which relates to an element of bidirectionality inherent in the migratory process. Sala (2017) argues that "the ability to identify with both cultures depends on how receptive the host culture is and what its political and social policies regarding cultural integration are" (p. 34).

Ward (2001), in her exploration of the psychological adaptation of migrant populations, identifies the strategies of assimilation and biculturalism available to migrants. Assimilation describes a person's "progress" towards identification with the culture of the destination country and distancing from the country of origin, which would be the goal of assimilation policies. Bukhori-Muslim (2015) in his research on young Australians of Indonesian origin describes assimilation as a process where the migrant minority totally embraces the culture of the country of destination and abandons its own. Progress would then be measured by how far migrants have come in their assimilation with the destination country (Ward, 2001). The second possible outcome is "biculturalism", which is achieved when migrants integrate but also keep "a balance between their home culture and that of the host" (Ward, 2001, p. 415).

Alternatively, Bukhori-Muslim (2015) describes the process of two cultures meeting as "counterbalancing" (a term which may also be used interchangeably with integration). Klingenberg et al. (2021) describe "counterbalancing" as a continuous process in which migrants negotiate integration and accommodation of the two cultures in order to establish a new identity. Once again, this outcome depends on the specific context in which migrants find themselves, emphasizing the role of the destination country. The notion of "counterbalancing" resembles the alternation model described by LaFromboise et al. (1993) as the process which makes it possible for a person to know and understand two different cultures. This dual cultural connection holds some mental health advantages for migrants. Psychological research exploring the relationship between mental health and immigration suggests that attachment to one's old culture may in fact be beneficial (Falicov, 2005). Maintaining one's traditional culture may serve as a buffer to the negative mental health effects that can arise from immigration (Marchetti-Mercer, 2017; Marchetti-Mercer & Roos, 2006; Vega et al., 1991, 1998).

Ward's (2001) "independent" model sees the migrant looking at the two countries as totally different domains. According to Bukhori-Muslim (2015), in this scenario migrants tend to keep to themselves and people from their own country of origin, separated from the dominant culture (Klingenberg et al., 2021), which may lead to the kind of "marginalization" described by Berry (2005).

Second- and third-generation processes of acculturation

The acculturation strategies adopted by second- and third-generation migrants may realistically be expected to follow a different social and psychological trajectory than those of their forebears.

Portes and Zhou (1993) have identified a process of "segmented assimilation" in the case of second generations and describe three possible scenarios, namely acculturation and integration into the dominant or majority middle class with concomitant economic success, preservation of original cultural practices, or downward mobility and acculturation into an underclass (Sala, 2017).

Portes and Rumbaut (2001) have explored the experiences of second-generation youth in the United States, and have identified three further types of acculturation, namely dissonant, consonant, and selective assimilation. Dissonant acculturation takes place when migrant youth adopt American ways, as well as the English language. However, their parents do not adapt at the same rate, which may lead to role reversal in the family, where parents become dependent on their children. Consonant acculturation occurs when acculturation takes place at the same time for both children and parents. This is most likely to occur amongst middle-class families. Lastly, there is selective acculturation, where the second generation becomes entrenched in a co-ethnic community which provides a source of support for the parents and reduces the loss of cultural norms and the mother tongue. This provides a buffer against the challenges of the migratory move for both parents and children (Levitt & Waters, 2002).

Marino (2019, 2021), in his exploration of the experiences of second- and third-generation Italians of Calabrese origin in Australia, describes evidence of a "double absence" in the second generation. This occurs when "individuals can be simultaneously considered 'foreigners' (or strangers) in their country of origin because they no longer live there, as well as in the dominant society, where metaphorically they do not really 'have a place'" (Marino, 2019, pp. 709–710). However, when it came to the third generation, he found that this group thought that "being Italian is cool" (Marino, 2019, p. 721). In other words, this group of participants seemed to perceive "markers of identity" such as a sense of style, fashion, food, and cooking as characteristic of Italian-ness very positively (Marino, 2019), perhaps reflecting the success of the recent "Made in Italy" marketing and brand. Verhaeghe et al. (2020) suggest that the assimilation of the third generation may be more "symbolic" in nature. This is in line with Gans's (1979) views on "symbolic ethnicity" – according to him, ethnicity in the second and third generations is only symbolic and not real and lies at the superficial level of cultural markers such as food and holidays. In our study, we interrogate the triviality potentially associated with this understanding of ethnicity in the discussion of our findings.

Transnationalism

Many of the theories that focus on migrants' adaptation have underplayed the relationship that migrants and their descendants retain with their country of origin and with family left behind. Hence, the concept of transnationalism may offer a useful understanding of the multidimensional experiences of migrant populations and succeeding generations. Vertovec (2009) suggests that transnationalism is an alternative way of looking at the experiences of current migrant populations, where "belonging, loyalty and a sense of attachment can be found and retained in more than one locality" (Klingenberg et al., 2021, p. 457). In this perspective, the emphasis is not on an "either/or" relationship between the destination country and the country of origin, but on how the relationship with the country of origin remains a powerful influence on the relationship with the destination country.

The concept of transnationalism began to gain prominence in the 1990s with the work of writers such as Schiller et al. (1992), who used the term to describe a new type of migrating population which has at its disposal networks, activities, and ways of life that reflect both the destination countries and the countries of origin (Marchetti-Mercer, 2017). A transnational perspective on migrant families implies that once migrants arrive in a new country, they do not necessarily abandon the familial and cultural links of the past. They maintain connections and commitments to both the country of origin and the destination country. This conceptual lens has also allowed researchers interested in the family experiences of migrants to foreground the role of the so-called "left-behind" family members in the life of migrants and the role they continue to play in migrants' lives (Baldassar, 2007; Marchetti-Mercer, 2017). Whilst the more traditional views on migration discussed earlier focused mostly on the challenges that migrants face once they arrive in a new country, they largely ignored the relationships that migrants continue to have with their country of origin, as well as the experiences of family left behind, sometimes referred as those who stay behind or as "non-migrant" family members (Marchetti-Mercer, 2012). According to Sala (2017), a transnational perspective allows a more nuanced understanding of what happens in terms of generational change, and acknowledges that, in the second generation, loss of the homeland culture and absorption into society in the destination country is not inescapable. Vertovec (1999) claims that transnationalism "has changed people's relations to space particularly by creating 'social fields' that connect and position some actors in more than one country" (p. 456). Klingenberg et al. (2021) see this as a dual orientation (p. 457) – referred to as "cosmopolitanism" by Vertovec (2009, p. 70) – which in practice offers the "cultural competence to manoeuvre through different systems socially" (Klingenberg et al., 2021, p. 458), as well as politically or economically (cf. Babar, 2016).

Sala (2017) underscores the work of McKay (2007), who argues that the role of the family in transnational studies has often been under-researched, whereas economic motives have been foregrounded. Thus, while transnationalism has often tended to be understood mainly from an economic or social point of view, it can also be understood from a more psychological and relational perspective, in what has been defined as "emotional transnationalism" (Falicov, 2007; Wolf, 2002). Cole and Groes (2016) speak of "affective circuits" to describe the circular relations between those who migrate and those who stay behind, and which are maintained, amongst other things, through emotions, people and goods. These circular relational and emotional interactions may be seen to lie at the root of the transnational experience (Marchetti-Mercer, 2017). Sala and Baldassar (2017) point out that emotional transnationalism is at the core of the second generation's experiences. They argue that it refers to an imaginary and emotionally based relationship with the land of their ancestors, which is mostly made possible through their parents' connections and attachments. This imaginary element was very much present in our participants' stories, and we therefore return to this topic later.

Undoubtedly, maintaining emotional connections between family members residing in different countries has been made easier by our living in a globalized world where international travel (despite the restrictions that the world faced during the COVID-19 pandemic) is reasonably easy and accessible. Furthermore, new information and communication technologies have made instant and immediate communication a reality for many people. No longer are phone calls reserved for special occasions because of the expense, and people no longer have to wait months to receive news from their loved ones. Through WhatsApp, and other social platforms, we are able to communicate frequently and fairly inexpensively. Emotional connections and relationships of care between those who migrate and those left behind are therefore possible in ways that could not be envisaged before (see, for example, Baldassar, 2007; Marchetti-Mercer & Swartz, 2020).

"Returning" to the country of origin

Emotional attachment to the country of origin may play a role in younger generations' "return" visits. For these generations, "returning" to the country of origin, the country of their forebears, seems to be a crucial factor in their own experiences of "home" and "belonging" (King & Christou, 2010). The search for "belonging" and "home" among the second generation "is often an extremely powerful, emotional, and even life-changing experience: an enactment of family heritage across time and space" (King & Christou, 2010, p. 109).

The idea of a "return" to the land of one's ancestors is a crucial concept in trying to understand the experiences of second- and third-generation immigrants. Baldassar (2001, 2011) describes the visits of second-generation Italians living in Australia to Italy as a kind of pilgrimage. Sala and Baldassar (2017) explore these visits as "a stage in the migration process and migrant life course", arguing "that life course effects are significant features of second-generation roots migration" (p. 389). Life course effects are still a relatively unexplored topic in the second-generation migration literature, but Conway and Potter (2009) also stress age and life course as critical demographic markers that influence such returns. Similarly, Levitt (2002), who researched transnational patterns among second-generation Irish, Dominican, and Indian immigrants in the United States maintains that "transnational practices do not remain constant across the life cycle. Instead, they ebb and flow at different stages, varying with the demands of work, school, and family" (p. 139). Levitt (2002) further found that her research participants tended to go back to their forebears' land of origin in early to middle adulthood and reported that their experiences of visits during their childhood played a role in eventual "roots" migration. Wessendorf (2007) similarly describes a process of "roots" migration in Swiss-born second-generation Italians back to Italy.

King and Christou (2010) point out that "in one sense 'return' is a misnomer, for many of these populations have not seen their 'homeland' for generations or centuries; indeed, they may not speak its language" (p. 105). Because of the impossibility of "return", these researchers prefer to speak of a "counter-diaspora", which they define "as the return of the second and subsequent generations to the diasporic hearth" (King & Christou, 2010, p. 115). However, despite this academic metaphor, children and grandchildren of the original diaspora who consider going to live in their ancestors' land conceptualize it as a "return".

Return and mobility

Findlay et al. (2015) argue that the field of migration studies has become increasingly attuned to the relationality of mobilities across time and space. Consequently, migration should not be seen as an individual single "event" at one point in time. Mobility must rather be seen as linking lives across time and space (Harris et al., 2020). This resonates with Falicov's (2007) view that migration affects not only the individual(s) who decide(s) to migrate, but also those left behind and the generations to come.

Recent literature on youth mobility has highlighted opportunities available to young people today regarding movement across borders (Harris et al.,

2020). This "mobility turn" in migration studies may be particularly relevant to the experiences of the younger third-generation participants of our study who have the means and tools at their disposal practically and psychologically to move easily between geographical spaces. According to Harris et al. (2020), the "youth mobilities" paradigm "challenge[s] not only linear and sedentarist notions of migrant acculturation and embeddedness over time but also binary spatial understandings of 'home' and host within transnational paradigms" (p. 4).

In line with this "mobility" lens, King and Christou (2010) have observed in the second-generation Greek immigrants that they studied a form of "return mobility". They explain: "Within (return) migration, there is a tension between mobility [...], and a search for a stable home(land) in which to settle and 'belong'" (p. 454).

The concept of a "diaspora"

To conclude this chapter, we would like to foreground the concept of a "diaspora", which is of particular relevance to our study. The concept has been explored through many theoretical lenses and went through several phases in its conceptualization. It was originally associated with the experiences of peoples dispersed from their country of origin following some traumatic event and regarded as victims (Clifford, 1994; Cohen, 2008; Helly, 2006).

Safran (1991) describes this type of diaspora in detail, regarding those in diaspora as "expatriate minority communities" with specific characteristics. These people (or their forebears) were driven by traumatic events from their original home to alien shores. They tend to "maintain a collective memory, which may be mythical, about their homeland" (King & Christou, 2010, p. 104), and they have a sense of separation because they believe that their destination country does not and will not accept them fully. They see their country of origin as their "true ideal" home, and dream that they or their descendants will eventually return there; hence they work to make this idealized homeland a safe and prosperous place. They also maintain a personal or vicarious connection to that "home" – this group's "consciousness and solidarity are defined by their ongoing relationship to their homeland" (King & Christou, 2010, p. 104).

Cohen (2008) developed a typology of diasporas that moves beyond a focus on victimhood; this typology may be more relevant to the Italian experience abroad, as it includes the example of the labour diaspora. In this instance, a diaspora is generated following emigration in search of work, as was evident in Italian migration especially in the late 19th and early 20th centuries. According to Cohen (2008), a diasporic consciousness develops if the migrant group that moves for work purposes maintains strong ties with the country of origin in respect of elements such as language, cultural norms, and religion, as well as a myth of, and connection to, the country of origin.

Gabaccia (2000, 2005) speaks of Italy's "diasporas" in the plural. This underlines the multiplicity of Italian people that have dispersed to different geographical areas, and that are influenced by assorted historical, political, and regional contexts (Sala, 2017). The plural acknowledges the multi-layeredness and complexity of migrant populations originating from the same country. This choice of terminology is of particular relevance in exploring the under-researched Italian immigrants in South Africa, as opposed to other groups in other parts of the world. Furthermore, the concept of plural Italian diasporas has sparked interest in the literary field. Notably, in 2020, Ganeri edited a special edition of the journal *Moderna*, entitled "Italian diaspora studies", which is the first attempt to reflect on the literature produced by Italians in different diasporic contexts; however, there is limited evidence of works written by Italians in South Africa.

A final construct relevant to our research is Lee's (2011) idea of an "intradiasporic transnationalism", which relates to the translocal ties that second- and third-generation immigrants may share with the children and grandchildren of other immigrants, rather than with family remaining in the country of origin. This term thus focuses on translocal connections between different population clusters within a single nation:

> Such ties can be an important means of maintaining a sense of belonging to a global 'nation' that has spread out from the original homeland and can involve a range of ties as complex and intense as those usually identified with host-home transnationalism.
>
> (Lee, 2011, p. 303)

Conclusion

In this chapter, we have provided a brief overview of the most salient concepts we used to understand the experiences of second- and third-generation Italians living in South Africa. The immigrant's position between the country of origin and destination country is a complex and multifaceted phenomenon. This point becomes evident in the next part of the book, where we discuss the most significant themes that arose from the analysis of our data.

References

Alba, R. (2005). Bright vs. blurred boundaries: Second-generation assimilation and exclusion in France, Germany, and the United States. *Ethnic and Racial Studies*, *28*(1), 20–49. https://doi.org/10.1080/0141987042000280003

Alba, R., & Nee, V. (1997). Rethinking assimilation theory for a new era of immigration. *International Migration Review*, *31*(4), 826–874. https://doi.org/10.1177/019791839703100403

34   *Theoretical context*

Andolfi, M. (2005). *La mediazione culturale. Tra l'estraneo e il familiare* (Vol. 36). Franco Angeli.

Andolfi, M. (2016). *Multi-generational family therapy: Tools and resources for the therapist.* Routledge. https://doi.org/10.4324/9781315545592

Babar, S. (2016). Burnt shadows: "Home", "cosmopolitanism" and "hybridization". *Journal of Humanities and Social Sciences, 24*(2), 109–126.

Baldassar, L. (2001). *Visits home: Migration experiences between Italy and Australia.* Melbourne University Press.

Baldassar, L. (2007). Transnational families and aged care: The mobility of care and the migrancy of ageing. *Journal of Ethnic and Migration Studies, 33*(2), 275–297. https://doi.org/10.1080/13691830601154252

Baldassar, L. (2011). Italian migrants in Australia and their relationship to Italy: Return visits, transnational caregiving and the second generation. *Journal of Mediterranean Studies, 20*(2), 255–282.

Baldassar, L. V., & Pesman, R. L. (2005). *From paesani to global Italians: Veneto migrants in Australia.* UWA Publishing.

Berry, J. W. (1992). Acculturation and adaptation in a new society. *International Migration, 30*(1), 69–85. https://doi.org/10.1111/j.1468-2435.1992.tb00776.x

Berry, J. W. (1997). Immigration, acculturation, and adaptation. *Applied Psychology, 46*(1), 5–34. https://doi.org/10.1111/j.1464-0597.1997.tb01087.x

Berry, J. W. (2001). A psychology of immigration. *Journal of Social Issues, 57*(3), 615–631. https://doi.org/10.1111/0022-4537.00231

Berry, J. W. (2005). Acculturation: Living successfully in two cultures. *International Journal of Intercultural Relations, 29*(6), 697–712. https://doi.org/10.1016/j.ijintrel.2005.07.013

Bourdieu, P. (2002). Habitus. In J. Hillier & E. Rooksby (Eds.), *Habitus: A sense of place* (pp. 27–34). Ashgate.

Bukhori-Muslim, A. (2015). *Acculturation, identification and hybridity: Cultural identity negotiation among young Australians of Indonesian origin* [Doctoral dissertation, Monash University]. https://doi.org/10.4225/03/58b38b062123a

Choate, M. I. (2012, March). Italy at home and abroad after150 years: The legacy of emigration and the future of *italianità. Italian Culture, 30*(1), 51–67. https://doi.org/10.1179/0161-462211Z.0000000001

Christou, A., & King, R. (2010). Imagining "home": Diasporic landscapes of the Greek-German second generation. *Geoforum, 41*(4), 638–646. https://doi.org/10.1016/j.geoforum.2010.03.001

Clifford, J. (1994). Diasporas. *Cultural Anthropology, 9*(3), 302–338. https://doi.org/10.1525/can.1994.9.3.02a00040

Cohen, R. (2008). *Global diasporas: An introduction* (2nd ed.). Routledge.

Cole, J., & Groes, C. (Eds.). (2016). *Affective circuits: African migrations to Europe and the pursuit of social regeneration.* University of Chicago Press.

Conway, D., & Potter, R. B. (2009). *Return migration of the next generations: 21st century transnational mobility.* Routledge. https://doi.org/10.4324/9781315244242

Di Nicola, V. (1997). *A stranger in the family: Culture, families, and therapy.* Norton.

Epstein, A. L. (1978). *Ethos and identity: Three studies in ethnicity.* Tavistock.

Falicov, C. J. (1995). Training to think culturally: A multidimensional comparative framework. *Family Process, 34*(4), 373–388. https://doi.org/10.1111/j.1545-5300.1995.00373.x

Falicov, C. J. (2005). Emotional transnationalism and family identities. *Family Process, 44*(4), 399–406. https://doi.org/10.1111/j.1545-5300.2005.00068.x

Falicov, C. J. (2007). Working with transnational immigrants: Expanding meanings of family, community, and culture. *Family Process, 46*(2), 157–171. https://doi.org/10.1111/j.1545-5300.2007.00201.x

Falicov, C. J. (2011). Migration and the family life cycle. In M. McGoldrick, B. Carter, & N. Garcia-Preto (Eds.), *The expanded family life cycle: Individual, family and social perspectives* (4th ed., pp. 336–347). Allyn & Bacon.

Findlay, A., McCollum, D., Coulter, R., & Gayle, V. (2015). New mobilities across the life course: A framework for analysing demographically linked drivers of migration. *Population, Space and Place, 21*(4), 390–402. https://doi.org/10.1002/psp.1956

Foucault, M. (1988a). Technologies of self. In L. Martin, H. Gutman, & P. Hutton (Eds.), *Technologies of the self: A seminar with Michel Foucault* (pp. 16–49). University of Massachusetts Press.

Foucault, M. (1988b). The political technology of individuals. In L. Martin, H. Gutman, & P. Hutton (Eds.), *Technologies of the self: A seminar with Michel Foucault* (pp. 145–162). University of Massachusetts Press.

Gabaccia, D. R. (2000). *Italy's many diasporas: Elites, exiles and workers of the world* (Global Diasporas series). Routledge.

Gabaccia, D. R. (2005). Juggling jargons: "Italians everywhere", diaspora or transnationalism? *Traverse, 1*, 49–64. https://www.e-periodica.ch/digbib/view?pid=tra-001:2005:1::223#51

Ganeri, M. (2020). Introduzione: L'imperativo globale degli *Italian diaspora studies. 22* (Moderna semestrale di teoria e di critica della letteratura), 9–16.

Gans, H. J. (1979). Symbolic ethnicity: The future of ethnic groups and cultures in America. *Ethnic and Racial Studies, 2*(1), 1–20. https://doi.org/10.1080/01419870.1979.9993248

Geertz, C. (1979). From the native's point of view: On the nature of anthropological understanding. In P. Rabinow & W. Sullivan (Eds.), *Interpretive social science* (pp. 225–242). University of California Press.

Gordon, M. M. (1961). Assimilation in America: Theory and reality. *Dædalus, 90*(2), 263–285.

Harris, A., Baldassar, L., & Robertson, S. (2020). Settling down in time and place? Changing intimacies in mobile young people's migration and life courses. *Population, Space and Place, 26*(8), e2357. https://doi.org/10.1002/psp.2357

Helly, D. (2006). Diaspora: History of an idea. In H. Moghissi (Ed.), *Muslim diaspora: Gender, culture and identity* (pp. 29–48). Routledge. https://doi.org/10.4324/9780203961254

Hirschman, C. (1983). America's melting pot reconsidered. *Annual Review of Sociology, 9*(August), 397–423. https://doi.org/10.1146/annurev.so.09.080183.002145

King, R., & Christou, A. (2010). Cultural geographies of counter-diasporic migration: Perspectives from the study of second-generation "returnees" to Greece. *Population, Space and Place, 16*(2), 103–119. https://doi.org/10.1002/psp.543

Klingenberg, A., Luetz, J. M., & Crawford, A. (2021). Transnationalism – Recognizing the strengths of dual belonging for both migrant and society. *Journal of International Migration and Integration, 22*(2), 453–470. https://doi.org/10.1007/s12134-020-00755-4

LaFromboise, T., Coleman, H. L., & Gerton, J. (1993, November). Psychological impact of biculturalism: Evidence and theory. *Psychological Bulletin, 114*(3), 395–412. https://doi.org/10.1037/0033-2909.114.3.395

Lee, H. (2011). Rethinking transnationalism through the second generation. *Australian Journal of Anthropology, 22*(3), 295–313. https://doi.org/10.1111/j.1757-6547.2011.00150.x

Levitt, P. (2002). The ties that change: Relations to the ancestral home over the lifecycle. In P. Levitt & M. C. Waters (Eds.), *The changing face of home: The transnational lives of the second generation* (pp. 123–144). Russell Sage Foundation.

Levitt, P., & Waters, M. C. (2002). Introduction. In P. Levitt & M. C. Waters (Eds.), *The changing face of home: The transnational lives of the second generation* (pp. 1–30). Russell Sage Foundation.

Marchetti-Mercer, M. C. (2006). New meanings of "home" in South Africa. *Acta Academica, 38*(2), 191–218.

Marchetti-Mercer, M. C. (2012). Those easily forgotten: The impact of emigration on those left behind. *Family Process, 51*(3), 373–383. https://doi.org/10.1111/j.1545-5300.2012.01407.x

Marchetti-Mercer, M. C. (2017). "The screen has such sharp edges to hug": The relational consequences of emigration in transnational South African emigrant families. *Transnational Social Work, 7*(1), 73–89. https://doi.org/10.1080/21931674.2016.1277650

Marchetti-Mercer, M. C., & Roos, J. L. (2006). Migration and exile – Some implications for mental health in post-apartheid South Africa. *South African Journal of Psychiatry, 12*(3), 52–64. https://doi.org/10.4102/sajpsychiatry.v12i3.67

Marchetti-Mercer, M. C., & Swartz, L. (2020). Familiarity and separation in the use of communication technologies in South African migrant families. *Journal of Family Issues, 41*(10), 1859–1884. https://doi.org/10.1177/0192513X19894367

Marino, S. (2019). Ethnic identity and race: The "double absence" and its legacy across generations among Australians of Southern Italian origin. Operationalizing institutional positionality. *Ethnic and Racial Studies, 42*(5), 707–725. https://doi.org/10.1080/01419870.2018.1451649

Marino, S. (2020). An intergenerational conceptualisation of Italian-Australian ethnic identity through Bourdieu and Heidegger. *Social Identities, 26*(1), 3–15. https://doi.org/10.1080/13504630.2019.1664286

Marino, S. (2021). Thrown into the world: The shift between pavlova and pasta in the ethnic identity of Australians originating from Italy. *Journal of Sociology, 57*(2), 231–248. https://doi.org/10.1177/1440783319888283

McGoldrick, M., Giordano, J., & Garcia-Preto, N. (2005). Ethnicity and family therapy. In M. McGoldrick, J. Giordano, & N. Garcia-Preto (Eds.), *Ethnicity and family therapy* (pp. 1–74). Guilford Press.

McKay, D. (2007). "Sending dollars shows feeling" – Emotions and economies in Filipino migration. *Mobilities, 2*(2), 175–194. https://doi.org/10.1080/17450100701381532

Parati, G., & Tamburry, A. J. (2011). Thinking anew: An introduction. In G. Parati & A. J. Tamburry (Eds.), *The cultures of Italian migration: Diverse trajectories and discrete perspectives* (pp. 1–7). Fairleigh Dickinson University Press.

Pierno, F. (2011). Building an identity on paper: The negotiation of *italianitá* in the early North American Ethnic Press. *Diasporas*, *19*, 91–99. https://doi.org/10.4000 /diasporas.1838

Portes, A., & Rumbaut, R. G. (2001). *Legacies: The story of the immigrant second generation*. University of California Press.

Portes, A., & Zhou, M. (1993). The new second generation: Segmented assimilation and its variants. *Annals of the American Academy of Political and Social Science*, *530*(1), 74–96. https://doi.org/10.1177/0002716293530001006

Raffaetà, R., Baldassar, L., & Harris, A. (2016). Chinese immigrant youth identities and belonging in Prato, Italy: Exploring the intersections between migration and youth studies. *Identities*, *23*(4), 422–437. https://doi.org/10.1080/1070289X.2015 .1024128

Reay, D. (1998). "Always knowing" and "never being sure": Familial and institutional habituses and higher education choice. *Journal of Education Policy*, *13*(4), 519– 529. https://doi.org/10.1080/0268093980130405

Safran, W. (1991). Diasporas in modern societies: Myths of homeland and return. *Diaspora: A Journal of Transnational Studies*, *1*(1), 83–99. https://doi.org/10.3138 /diaspora.1.1.83

Sala, E. (2017). *The Italian-ness is in the family: A critical evaluation of the role of family in constructions of ethnicity and connections to homeland among two cohorts of second generation Italian-Australians* [Doctoral dissertation, PhD thesis, University of Western Australia]. https://api.research-repository.uwa.edu.au /ws/portalfiles/portal/20507794/THESIS_DOCTOR_OF_PHILOSOPHY_SALA _Emanuela_2017.pdf

Sala, E., & Baldassar, L. (2017). Leaving family to return to family: Roots migration among second-generation Italian-Australians. *Ethos*, *45*(3), 386–408. https://doi .org/10.1111/etho.12173

Schiller, N. G., Basch, L., & Blanc-Szanton, C. (1992). Transnationalism: A new analytic framework for understanding migration. *Annals of the New York Academy of Science*, *645*(1), 1–24. https://doi.org/10.1111/j.1749-6632.1992.tb33484.x

Vega, W. A., Kolody, B., Aguilar-Gaxiola, S., Alderete, E., Catalano, R., & Caraveo-Anduaga, J. (1998). Lifetime prevalence of DSM-III-R psychiatric disorders among urban and rural Mexican Americans in California. *Archives of General Psychiatry*, *55*(9), 771–778. https://doi.org/10.1001/archpsyc.55.9.771

Vega, W. A., Kolody, B., Valle, R., & Weir, J. (1991). Social networks, social support, and their relationship to depression among immigrant Mexican women. *Human Organization*, *50*(2), 154–162. https://doi.org/10.17730/humo.50.2 .p340266397214724

Verhaeghe, F., Bradt, L., Van Houtte, M., & Derluyn, I. (2020). Identificational assimilation patterns in young first, second, 2.5 and third-generation migrants. *Young*, *28*(5), 502–522. https://doi.org/10.1177/110330881990072

Vertovec, S. (1999). Conceiving and researching transnationalism. *Ethnic and Racial Studies*, *22*(2), 447–462. https://doi.org/10.1080/014198799329558

Vertovec, S. (2009). *Transnationalism*. Routledge.

Viola, L., & Verheul, J. (2019). The media construction of Italian identity: A Transatlantic, digital humanities analysis of *italianità*, ethnicity, and whiteness, 1867–1920. *Identity*, *19*(4), 294–312. https://doi.org/10.1080/15283488.2019 .1681271

Ward, C. (2001). The A, B, C of acculturation. In D. Matsumoto (Ed.), *The handbook of culture and psychology* (pp. 411–515). Oxford University Press.

Wessendorf, S. (2007). "Roots migrants": Transnationalism and "return" among second-generation Italians in Switzerland. *Journal of Ethnic and Migration Studies, 33*(7), 1083–1102. https://doi.org/10.1080/13691830701541614

Wessendorf, S. (2016). *Second-generation transnationalism and roots migration: Cross-border lives.* Routledge.

Wolf, D. L. (2002). There's no place like "home": Emotional transnationalism and the struggles of second-generation Filipinos. In P. Levitt & M. C. Waters (Eds.), *The changing face of home: The transnational lives of the second generation* (pp. 255–294). Russell Sage Foundation.

4 Historical context of the Italian community

Introduction

In order to understand the identity construction of second- and third-generation Italian immigrants in South Africa, it is helpful to look at the origins of this community. It is, we believe, a unique history, quite different from those of the Americas, Australia, and European countries. The migration of Italians to South Africa was scattered over a long time, and immigrants came from many geographical locations, not only in Italy but also from other parts of the African continent. Furthermore, although there was an Italian presence in South Africa prior to World War II, it was only after 1945 that the numbers of the Italian community increased considerably, primarily because Italian prisoners of war sent to South Africa decided to stay in the country, or to return, despite repatriation, after the end of the war. In 1924, only 1,721 Italians were recorded to be living in the (then) four provinces of South Africa, whereas in the 1970s, the numbers exceeded 50,000 (Briani, 1980).

Italian immigration to South Africa prior to World War II

Although the presence of Italians before World War II was numerically limited, their history has not gone unnoticed. Nor is it made up of anonymous individuals whose names have been lost – quite the opposite in fact. It is not a history of large waves of Italian immigrants, but one consisting of stories of small groups or individuals, who in different ways distinguished themselves and are still remembered today.

As early as the late 17th century, there was an Italian presence at the southern tip of Africa. At that time, some *Valdesi* (Waldensians) from the Piedmont region in the north of Italy joined the original Dutch settlers and their descendants (who were later called the *Boere*, from the Dutch word for farmers, or Boers, in the anglicized form) in their spread into southern Africa, united by their common Protestant religious beliefs. These Waldensians fled religious persecution in Europe by the Roman Catholic Church between 1688 and 1689 (Marchetti-Mercer & Virga, 2021). One and a half centuries later, in 1838, Teresa Viglione, a Piedmontese *valdese*, became famous for

DOI: 10.4324/9781003266884-4

saving a large group of Voortrekkers (descendants of the original Dutch colonists who decided to migrate north from the Cape Colony to other parts of southern Africa to escape British colonial rule) from an imminent Zulu attack against them. Viglione was able to warn the Maritz camp of Voortrekkers before the Zulus could reach them after she rode from the Italian encampment near where the initial attacks occurred (Selby, 1973) and she was honoured for her heroism by the Afrikaner nation, who immortalized her in a frieze in the Voortrekker Monument in Pretoria (Marchetti-Mercer & Virga, 2021).

Other small groups of Italians arrived in South Africa around the end of the 19th century and at the start of the 20th century. One of these was a group of Sicilian fishermen who settled in the Cape Colony. By 1910, a total of 70 of these fishermen were recorded in this region (Sani, 1992). A remarkable group came from Avigliana, in Piedmont, to Modderfontein, Johannesburg, in 1890 to work in a dynamite factory requiring delicate wrapping of dynamite. This is an intriguing story, as all these workers, known in Italian as *cartucciere*, were women. They were followed by more women workers. Another well-known group was comprised of 32 people – families with children and some single men – from Lombardy, commemorated as protagonists in Dalene Matthee's well-known novel *The Mulberry Forest* (1987). They settled in the Gouna's forests near Knysna, on the southern coast, hoping to farm silkworms. They brought their own silkworms to start the business, only to discover, once on site, that the local mulberry trees were not suited to feed and breed their silkworms.

In the years between 1899 and 1902, the South African War (formerly known as the Anglo-Boer War) was fought primarily between the British and the two Boer Republics, the Transvaal (the Zuid-Afrikaansche Republiek) and the Orange Free State (Oranje Vrijstaat). The Italians mostly sided with the Boers. A famous Italian linked to this conflict is Captain Ricchiardi, who formed the Italian Volunteer Legion in support of the Boers (Sani, 1992; Marchetti & Virga, 2021). The Boer Republics were forced to capitulate at the end of May 1902, despite continued resistance, and all of southern Africa came under British rule.

When South Africa obtained limited independence from Britain and the Union of South Africa was established in 1910, the new country required the construction of strategic and symbolic buildings and infrastructure. A number of Italians were involved in constructing of the Union Buildings (the administrative building for the new government) in Pretoria in 1913, extensions of the Cape Town harbour, and the Voortrekker Monument in Pretoria between 1939 and 1949 (Marchetti-Mercer & Virga, 2021).

Italian immigrants, like many other Europeans, were also attracted to South Africa at the end of the 19th century by the discovery of diamonds around Kimberly in the then northern Cape Colony, and of gold in the Witwatersrand, including the area which is today the city of Johannesburg.

However, this immigration was unstable; many of these fortune-hunters did not settle permanently.

Despite these relatively small numbers, there is evidence that an Italian presence was starting to take root in the country, as is shown by the foundation of Italian associations. In 1890, the first Italian association, the Italian Mutual Aid and Charitable Society, was founded in Cape Town; in 1909, a similar association, the Italian Union, was established in Johannesburg. Shortly thereafter, welfare associations and educational associations began to establish themselves, a sign of the desire and determination of the Italian community not only to help each other but also to ensure the local preservation of the Italian language and culture. In 1908, an after-school centre was founded in Cape Town to teach Italian to the community's children with the financial support of Luigi Fatti from Johannesburg (Bini, 1957). Fatti, who left Italy in 1866, opened a grocery store in Johannesburg in 1896. His rivals were the Moni brothers, Pietro and Giacomo, who founded their own company ten years later. Many decades later, in 1982, however, these two companies merged to become Fatti's & Moni's, a brand that still exists and is associated with pasta products. Fatti also established an Italian school for his employees' children in Johannesburg in the early 1920s. This school subsequently became the Dante Alighieri Society, officially founded in October of 1927.

The Dante Alighieri Society, which today has four branches in South Africa and a history of almost a century, is a point of reference for Italians and their descendants who want to learn Italian. A formal Italian school, with a complete Italian curriculum, has never been founded in South Africa, so the Dante Alighieri Society has been the institution that has had to compensate for the absence of such a school. Many of the participants in our research mentioned that they attended the Dante Society to learn Italian as children, or as a place where they would like to go to learn Italian. Antonio, for example, whose father moved to South Africa after World War II, decided to improve his language skills by going to the Dante: "*And obviously, you know, you pick up a few words here and there from what they would say. But obviously it's a completely different structure, so my sister and I both decided to enrol at Dante Alighieri at the beginning of last year.*" Carla describes going to "*the Dante*" as a child, "*for like maybe a couple of years, and it was like the very basic things*". This experience was shared by Federico and other participants, whose parents wanted them to learn Italian. Therefore, when it comes to the language education of the children of Italian families, the Dante Alighieri Society still maintains its role as a reference point for the Italian community in South Africa.

World War II and Zonderwater

During World War II, Italian soldiers captured in North Africa and in the Italian colonies on the Horn of Africa (Somalia, Eritrea, and Ethiopia) were sent as prisoners of war to South Africa, which was not only geographically far away from the areas in which the conflict was taking place but had not been devastated by the war, although curfews, blackouts, and food and fuel rationing applied. The most famous prisoner of war camp where Italians were sent was Zonderwater, in Cullinan, about 50 km from the administrative capital city of Pretoria. Between 1941 and 1947, Zonderwater housed more than 100,000 Italian prisoners of war, making it the largest single camp to house such prisoners, and it had the dimensions of a small town. This camp proved to be quite different from other prisoner of war camps, possibly because of the leadership of the camp commandant, Colonel Prinsloo, who managed the camp in a very enlightened way. The prisoners were treated with dignity and were granted many freedoms and opportunities usually denied to prisoners of war. Gazzini (1987), one of the internees, author of one of the most remarkable memoirs of the Zonderwater years, wrote:

> Era in atto il lodevole tentativo [...] di non spegnere la personalità del recluso, bensì, per quanto possibile, di valorizzarla. Zonderwater non era il paradiso, ma per chi veniva dall'inferno, poteva anche sembrarlo (pp. 13–14). [It was in fact a laudable attempt [...] not to extinguish the personality of the prisoner but rather as far as possible to value it, Zonderwater was not paradise but for those who came from hell, it might have seemed like it] (own translation).

According to another memoir, by Captain John Ball, who was one of the officers responsible for the camp, "art, theatre, and music formed a pre-eminent part of camp life" and "some 9,000 P.O.W. who, when taken captive were illiterate, learned to read and write their mother tongue, Italian, at Zonderwater" (Ball, 1967, n. p.). Annese (2010) and Kruger (1996) report plenty of cultural, entertainment and sporting activities for the Italian prisoners to participate in. After the Armistice between Italy and the Allies on 8 September 1943, prisoners who formally renounced fascism were no longer considered enemies, and were allowed to work outside the camp. At this time, many Italians became known to the local population, and, in turn, the Italians learned to appreciate the country in which they found themselves. After the war, around 1,000 former prisoners of war were granted permission to remain in South Africa, and over 1,000 returned after their initial repatriation to Italy (Van Graan, 2021), making this the largest influx of Italian immigrants to South Africa. Indeed, as Sani (1992) argues, it is possible that the repatriated former prisoners of war who subsequently returned to South Africa convinced other Italians in their homeland to emigrate to this southern African country.

The importance of the former Italian prisoners of war as a group of immigrants lies in the numbers. Moreover, for the first time in the history of Italian migration to South Africa, such a large number of Italians came from a shared experience. By contrast, as we have seen, previously (and even later), Italian immigration tended to consist of single individuals or small scattered groups.

Here we see the immigration of thousands of Italians from different origins but united by the same fate – of having been Zonderwater prisoners. Not surprisingly, then, Zonderwater has become a prominent symbol to the Italian community in South Africa. Somma (2007), in his postgraduate research on the music produced at Zonderwater, argues that "the memorialising of these prisoners is central to the validation of identity for this community [the Italians in South Africa]" (p. 3). In a later study, he also speaks of the "generative mythos of the Italian POW experience" (Somma, 2013, p. 167). The area where the camp stood has been preserved as a place of remembrance. There is a cemetery where approximately 250 of the soldiers who died during their imprisonment are buried. There are also a museum and a monument, the "Three Arches", which is a symbol of the camp. Every year, on the first Sunday in November, members of the Italian community, in the presence of the highest institutional Italian officials in South Africa and members of the South African armed forces, meet for a ceremony in memory of the prisoners of war.

This story, regardless of whether individual members of the community have personal or family ties with Zonderwater, holds a special place in the narrative of the founding of the Italian community in South Africa, but outside the Italian community, this history is relatively unknown (Van Graan, 2021). This lack of awareness outside the Italian community may be one reason for Zonderwater's centrality in the collective identity of Italians in South Africa. It is a story that concerns the relations between the two countries and their peoples, but the fact that it is not widely known outside the Italian community makes it even more "intimate" and almost "exclusive" to Italians in South Africa.

Today, in the Italian community, it is common to find descendants of the Italian prisoners of war at Zonderwater. In our study, Sandra and Susanna, for example, were granddaughters of one of the former prisoners of war, who was still alive at the time of the interview. Sandra recounted that when the time came for her grandfather to be repatriated, he

> decided to stay here, so when … they wanted, they called them all back to Italy, they came to fetch them and he hid in the toilets in those long drops. […] he refused to come; they didn't see him, he hid there and then he just … he had nothing, he was literally poor, he had the shirt on his back. And then he just did odd jobs for people … and that's how he came to be here.

Angelo also shared that his grandfather had migrated to South Africa when he was a teenager because his uncle had been a prisoner of war at Zonderwater.

Ignazio recalled that his grandfather spent some time in Zonderwater, but he was later moved to another prisoners' camp, in Worcester, in the Cape. After the war, he decided to remain in South Africa:

He stayed after the war. He [...] didn't have very much, I don't know, in those days, it was very difficult to communicate [...] back home and there was no communication between them, between him and his family for about 10 years or 20 years. And then they came over and it was apparently a big thing; it was in the papers and everything because he connected with his family after ... 15 years or something like that.

The post-war years and apartheid South Africa

According to Sani (1992), in 1947, only 945 Italians relocated to South Africa, even though Italian emigration abroad after World War II was very common, as many fled war-ravaged Italy. When the National Party came into power in South Africa in 1948, restrictions were put in place to limit European immigration and to promote the interests of the local white Afrikaner population in order to "preserve" the white minority in the country. Glaser (2010) explains:

Once the Nationalists were in power [...] only Dutch and German immigrants, who were deemed more likely to integrate into Afrikaner society, were welcomed. So, in spite of the perceived demographic vulnerability of whites and in spite of a growing skilled labour shortage, the Nationalist government imposed a highly restrictive European immigration regime between 1949 and 1960.

(p. 66)

The year 1948 also marked the start of the South African government's implementation of its policies of racial segregation, known as apartheid. These policies institutionalized racial discrimination, creating an unequal society where the white minority was privileged, while the black majority was severely disadvantaged. According to Peberdy (2009), there is also evidence of discrimination against immigrants who were likely to be Roman Catholic from southern Europe in the 1960s and 1970s, which would have included Italians, while the admission of Protestant immigrants was facilitated.

Despite these restrictive measures and official suspicion towards white Catholics, who were perceived as somehow different from other whites, Italians living in South Africa still enjoyed the rights and privileges of the white minority. Many important and well-known Italian enterprises opened branches in South Africa in the 1950s and 1960s, including Fiat, Olivetti, Iveco, and Alitalia. One of our participants, Beatrice, was the daughter of an Olivetti worker. She recalled her father travelling *"around the country a lot because he was fixing and teaching about typewriters"*. Charles's uncle, who was originally a Franciscan priest, left the Church to work at Olivetti. Marcelle's father held a senior position at Alitalia.

The local mines continued to attract migrants, including many Italians. In the East Rand, just outside Johannesburg, many Italians were employed at the

East Rand Property Mines company, one of the deepest mines in the world (Marchetti-Mercer & Virga, 2021). One of our participants, Tullio, recalled that his father was a miner at Crown Mines in Gauteng:

> My father saw an ad in the newspaper, things were tough in Italy and there was an ad in the paper to come to the mines. Free passage on the ship, board and lodging, food, pay for studying and a three-year contract and give you money to go. [...] that is how they came. And that's [how] a whole bunch of Italians came. [...] And they all arrived in Johannesburg, many of them worked at Crown Mines where my father befriended a whole lot of other Italians. They used to socialize at the Italian club.

In the 1950s many Italian clubs were founded as social spaces for the community in various South African cities or re-established after having been put in abeyance during the war, as in the case of the Circolo Sociale Italiano in Cape Town (Sani, 1992). Many of these clubs and associations still exist today.

In this period, other Italians also arrived in South Africa, following other migration paths. As mentioned earlier, one of the peculiarities of the history of Italian immigration to South Africa is that many Italians came from other African countries, rather than directly from Italy. A large group of these came from the former colony of Eritrea, whence they fled during World War II, under British occupation. However, some of them remained in that country, and only left after Eritrea was annexed by Ethiopia and the civil war broke out. Most of the Italians lived in the capital city, Asmara (Podestà, 2019) – for this reason, this group of immigrants from Eritrea to South Africa is known as *Asmarini*. Some of them were born in Eritrea, and, even though they maintained a strong relationship with Italy and retained language competency in Italian, they had in fact never lived in Italy. Therefore, when they had to leave Eritrea, they chose to relocate to South Africa rather than to Italy in order to remain on the African continent. On 1 July 1970, they established the CIAO, the Circolo Italiano Africa Orientale. Lilla was one of our participants whose grandmother was born in Eritrea. Lilla's grandparents met in Eritrea, and they both relocated to South Africa, where Lilla's mother was born.

Some of the *Asmarini* did not come directly to South Africa after leaving Eritrea. Like other Italians, they first travelled through other African countries before finding a final home in South Africa. Dario, for example, told us that his father's side of the family lived in what was then Rhodesia (now Zimbabwe), whereas his mother's side lived in Zambia, before they all moved to Rhodesia (Zimbabwe) and from there to South Africa in 1980. In Diego's case, his father worked for a few years in Mozambique in the 1950s, before settling in South Africa. Laura's grandparents moved from Torino to Tanzania after World War II, and her father was born there. In other instances, before arriving in South Africa, Italian migrants had therefore already had previous experience of living in an African country; for example, Giulia's grandfather lived first in Rhodesia (Zimbabwe), then went back to Italy, and finally relocated to South Africa. These different migratory paths are unique to the Italian diaspora in South Africa. They are not isolated cases – they are common to many Italians here, who despite having maintained a strong bond with Italy, have evidently built their own Italian identity in a more general diaspora in Africa. South Africa, therefore, seems to function as a final destination of these dispersed Italian identities.

Many of our younger participants from both the second and third generations were born in the 1980s and 1990s, the two decades that saw the end of the apartheid regime. In the 1980s, international pressure to end apartheid escalated. Pressure was exerted, among other things, through various economic and cultural sanctions and embargos against South Africa. Italy, albeit in a somewhat ambivalent way (Ercolessi, 2015), participated in these actions, but this resulted only in a partial withdrawal of Italian investments from the country until the first democratic election in 1994. This inconsistency is evident from the fact that, in 1983, at the height of international sanctions, the Italian-South African Chamber of Trade and Industries was founded to promote business partnerships between South Africa and Italy. According to Fiamingo (2015), the Italian government was afraid that there might be a rise in communism in the southern African region and was therefore not prepared to oppose the South African apartheid regime fully, because it had strong anti-communism policies.

Concluding remarks

As we have seen from this brief overview of the history of Italian immigration to South Africa, politics linked to race, nationality, and religion has always played a major role in shaping the fate of immigrants to this country. This has ranged from a lesser to a greater level of social acceptance, and to policies explicitly for or against the immigration of people from specific parts of the world. The same issues continue to shape South African immigration policies today. These policies challenge not only new immigrants but also earlier immigrants and their descendants in articulating their sense of "belonging" and finding a "home", as we show in the last part of this book.

References

Annese, C. (2010). *I diavoli di Zonderwater. 1941–1947. La storia dei prigionieri italiani in Sudafrica che sopravvissero alla guerra grazie allo sport.* Sperling & Kupfer.

Ball, J. A. (1967). Italian prisoners of war in South Africa 1941–1947. *Military History Journal, 1*(1). https://www.samilitaryhistory.org/vol011jb.html

Bini, A. (1957). *Italiani in Sud Africa.* Scuole Arti Gra che Artigianelli.

Briani, V. (1980). *Il lavoro Italiano in Africa.* Tipografia riservata del Ministero degli affari esteri.

Ercolessi, M. C. (2015). Italy and apartheid South Africa: Between innovation and ambivalence, 1976–1990. In A. Lissoni & A. Pezzano (Eds.), *The ANC between home and exile: Reflections on the anti-apartheid struggle in Italy and Southern Africa* (pp. 37–52). Università degli Studi Napoli, "L'Orientale" – Dipartimento Asia, Africa e Mediterraneo.

Fiamingo, C. (2015). The anti-apartheid movement in Italy: Processes, mechanisms and heritage. In A. Lissoni & A. Pezzano (Eds.), *The ANC between home and exile. Reflections on the anti-apartheid struggle in Italy and southern Africa* (pp. 53–80). Università degli Studi Napoli, "L'Orientale" – Dipartimento Asia, Africa e Mediterraneo.

Gazzini, M. (1987). *Zonderwater. I prigionieri in Sudafrica (1941–1947)*. Bonacci Editore.

Glaser, C. (2010). Portuguese immigrant history in twentieth century South Africa: A preliminary overview. *African Historical Review, 42*(2), 61–83. https://doi.org/10.1080/17532523.2010.517398

Kruger, C. (1996). The Zonderwater Italian prisoners of war 1941–1947: Fifty years down the line. *South African Journal of Cultural History, 10*(2), 88–104. https://hdl.handle.net/10520/AJA10113053_189

Marchetti-Mercer, M. C., & Virga, A. (2021). The Italian diaspora in South Africa: Origins and identity. *Italian Studies.* https://doi.org/10.1080/00751634.2021.1923174

Matthee, D. (1987). *The mulberry forest.* Penguin.

Peberdy, S. A. (2009). *Selecting immigrants: Nationalism and national identity in South Africa's immigration policies, 1910 to 1998.* Wits University Press.

Podestà, G. L. (2019). *L'emigrazione italiana in Africa orientale.* http://www.ilcornodafrica.it/rds-01emigrazione.pdf

Sani, G. (1992). *History of the Italians in South Africa 1489–1989.* Zonderwater Block.

Selby, J. (1973). *A short history of South Africa.* Routledge.

Somma, D. A. (2007). *Mythologising music: Identity and culture in the Italian prisoner of war camps of South Africa* [Master's dissertation, University of the Witwatersrand]. https://issuu.com/zonderwater/docs/tesi_di_donato_andrew_somma_su_zonderwater

Somma, D. A. (2013). *Italian prisoners of war in the South African imagination: Contemporary memory, history and narrative* [PhD thesis, University of the Witwatersrand]. https://issuu.com/zonderwater/docs/italian_prisoners_of_war_in_the_sou

Van Graan, M. (2021, March). History and literature: Magic realism and Italian POWs in a South African novel. *Journal of Literary Studies/Tydskrif vir Literatuurwetenskap, 37*(1), 86–103. https://doi.org/10.1080/02564718.2021.1887654

5 "Our family does everything together"

The importance of the family of origin

Introduction

The family of origin plays a crucial role in the process of cultural transmission to second- and third-generation migrants. These experiences can best be understood through a transgenerational family lens which underscores the role that the family of origin plays in shaping the cultural identity of an individual via the transmission of relevant norms and values (McGoldrick et al., 2005). In the intimate space of the family of origin, parents and grandparents impart the most essential elements of their own experience of culture and their sense of connection to their country of origin to the younger generations.

As discussed in Chapter 3, the family is essentially the first place where we get a sense of home, as well as what it means to belong to a certain group. It is our first immersion in the "culture" of our ancestors. This sense of "culture" can speak to different elements of our lives: the language(s) we speak, the values and norms we hold dear, the foods we eat, the rituals we adhere to, our religious affiliation and the practices we follow, and even the sports teams we support (Marchetti-Mercer, 2006). In immigrant families, these transgenerational narratives are often filled with nostalgic tales of the "old country", often providing a fairly idealized picture of what has been left behind.

In this context, one should be careful not to speak in an essentialist way of one universal "Italian culture" or to assume that all Italian families are the same, even in Italy. The danger of overgeneralizing the cultural norms of a specific ethnic group became evident in the initial criticism aimed at McGoldrick et al.'s first version of the book *Ethnicity and Family Therapy*, which was published in 1982. This original volume consisted of specific individual chapters describing the kind of familial depictions and behaviours claimed to be most likely in different cultural groups such as Italians, the Irish, and others. These descriptions were often presented without sufficient critical reflection on the implications of generalizing purported cultural and ethnic characteristics. (Subsequent editions have paid attention to this problem.) Furthermore, it is important to note that individual families also tend to develop their own unique "culture" (Di Nicola, 1997), or adopt norms that are often a product of many transgenerational processes and transmissions. Instead of thinking in terms of specific groups or entities, our book responds to Falicov's (1995) call

DOI: 10.4324/9781003266884-5

to understand how common human experiences are approached by diverse groups of people, in line with Marchetti-Mercer's (2006) study.

The role of the family of origin

As we have discussed in the section on *italianità* in Chapter 3, there is a risk of stereotyping the concept of the "Italian family" – here we do not wish to idealize the idea of "the family" in general, or the "Italian family" in particular. In this regard, Sala and Baldassar (2017) note that the concept of family has traditionally played an important role in the identity of Italian immigrants, but they simultaneously and justifiably emphasize that this "idealized view" is not always realistic.

Many of our participants mentioned the role that their families played in their lives. Gabriella commented: *"There's more of a family orientation. Like I'm very family-oriented here."* Diego spoke expansively on how close and integrated his family experience was when he was a child:

> You know, if I think of when I grew up as a kid, I identified – if I think back – very, very much [with] the family unit. Very, you know, the kids were part of everything. We weren't told to go and play there or go and play there. The kids were part of it, and the moms and the dads and everybody would be carrying on and when you were tired you would go and [lie] down.

In some instances, participants mentioned how they were exposed to traditional family values while growing up:

> So my brother and I have both been brought up to love and respect and be affectionate towards people. Hugs, hallo, like kisses goodbye, that kind of thing. … also yes we are very much involved in the Italian community because of our parents and grandparents; we have learned all the traditions of cooking and the traditional meals … the way we have lunch.
>
> (Marina)

Other participants also emphasized this – *"[a]nd so having those values, you know, and also the typical Christian values … , love your parents, … Family values"* (Nino) and *"[f]amily because they value that a lot. The tradition, obviously, everything they do"* (Gabriella).

It may well be that the prominence given to tradition is something residual from their forebears' past, as Laura herself wondered: *"I think always growing up, it's always the values. So, I think – it's going to sound weird – but they're like very tradition … conservative traditional values seem to characterize Italians here. I don't know if it's the same in Italy."* One may speculate that the original migrants brought with them more traditional values linked to their own permanence in Italy in the first half of the last century, and these were then passed on to the younger generations. This was echoed in Lilla's experiences:

> So because it's a place in time that my grandparents moved here which was the [19]50s, ... conservative values and they've imposed those values on their children, and so my parents carried that on, whereas my mom looks at some of her cousins in Italy and those values are not exactly the same.

One thing that was intriguing in our participants' stories is that we did not see any evidence of opposition to these traditional family values in the second and third generations. Nor did participants recount challenging their parents' attachment to Italy. This seems to contrast with what has been reported in some other research (for example, Falicov, 2007), which has shown that younger generations of immigrant families often prefer to assimilate into the dominant culture and may reject the values of their forebears, often bringing about intergenerational conflict.

Some participants expressed pride in certain qualities which they believed were inherently linked to "being Italian", such as the idea that Italians are "hard workers". Matteo expressed this as follows: *"I am so proud of the fact that my father and my mother came here from Italy, and they were, because of the Italian ... because of being Italian they were able to come here, work hard, sacrifice."* This was also emphasized by Alberto:

> and obviously I think just that sense of hard work. I think that was something that was instilled from my grandparents from a very early age; [it] is just that they came here with essentially absolutely nothing and they really did make successes of themselves and I think to a large extent throughout the whole Italian community in South Africa at least. ... So I think those are the two qualities I really do get, and that we're not a nation of people that are afraid of hard work and we do look out for one another.

The importance of rituals and religious feasts in Italian families' lives, especially those linked to events such as Christmas and Easter, was also stressed. Matteo recalled: *"We follow all the Italian traditions, even when it's San [...], or San Vincenzo, then my mother will phone me and say hey today it is San Vincenzo, because that is my second name."* This was also part of Angelo's experience: *"Christmas, Easter ... my grandmother was very Catholic obviously so it was different, various days attributed to Saints and all of that kind of thing, mostly just Christmas and Easter, ja."* Alberto remembered:

> We do the Sunday lunch and something small, ... we are never away over Easter or Christmas, we always do that at home. Small stuff like

that, it just stays with you … it's a tie that just brings everyone back together. Specifically obviously around the religious holidays.

Silvio recounted that *"over the festive seasons and over Easter we are very tight and over birthdays of course. [...] interestingly the whole Saint Day thing"*. Marina confirmed that her *"family does everything together; so confirmations, holy communions, birthdays ... Yes, the traditional Italian way of kind of being with family and Christmas is huge"*.

These experiences echo the views of Walsh (2009), who notes the importance of rituals in the lives of families, explaining that "rituals and ceremonies carry profound significance, connecting individuals and families with their larger community, its history, and its survival over adversity" (p. 5). Falicov (2009) points out the "power of rituals to restore continuity with a family's heritage" (p. 201), which is particularly relevant to immigrant families. One can argue that rituals function as a performative aspect of families' cultural identities, and these often take the form of family gatherings and celebrations (Sala, 2017). Falicov (2009) also stresses the role of religion in the lives of migrants, because it

[c]an provide internal continuity and transportability of beliefs and practices both in the privacy of one's mind or home and in the public area of the church. In so doing, religious activity can reaffirm ethnicity in a new context as something valued and respected.

(p. 165)

Religious celebrations in the context of the family were indeed very evident in the experiences of the majority of our participants.

The uniqueness of Italian values and traditions was often juxtaposed with South African Anglophone culture, especially in the case where participants had non-Italian partners. This was experienced as a challenge in the sense that these participants often felt that their partners lacked a true understanding of their Italian-ness:

And I tell you my father, he was proper Italian, he said try whatever you do and marry a Mediterranean. He says I would like you to marry Italian, but in South Africa, we know it's hard, so try and marry at least a Mediterranean because he will understand you better. And it is so true. I have married an English[-speaking] man. He doesn't understand. He says I am always stressed, but I am not stressed, okay. He says you are always so stressed, you are like a whirlwind. I said, but … he says you are so emotional and … but I am not. That is me.

(Donatella)

Sandra also described clashes with her husband: *"It is, it is. It's a huge clash, ja, his family is very British and very English, very stiff upper lip, I think that's why he married me, he was rebelling."* However, in the case of Susanna, her non-Italian husband embraced Italian culture:

> He loved it. He has been to Italy before because he studied Latin in school and so they went on a Latin tour to Italy ... And he loves the Italian, he has actually got an aptitude for it. He can, I mean, he has had no background with it, but he already can pick [it] up and understand.

Notably grandparents were identified by both the second- and third-generation participants as central to their family life, and as the primary transmitters of Italian culture. Angelo said: *"But I felt more that I wasn't getting handed down my heritage from my mom so much as my grandparents."* This comment is in line with the findings of Papadopoulos (2002), who describes grandparents in migrant families as the "holders of the traditional values and customs of the home country" (p. 37).

Consequently, when grandparents passed away, there was also a loss of connection with Italy, as Sandra lamented: *"[S]adly, you know, my grandparents are all dead except for one but she is not right in her mind. You know, that time is slipping away, and that whole Italian-ness that we had, which centred around my grandparents, is now gone."* Grandparents may also both consciously and unconsciously transfer their sense of nostalgia for Italy to the next generations, perhaps in an attempt to maintain their sense of hope with regard to a real or imagined return.

However, this sense of connection of the migrants with Italy may at times be ruptured, affecting the second and third generations. This was the case of Lara, whose Italian-born father felt little loyalty towards his land of birth because of his experiences in post–World War II Italy. Lara ascribed her limited cultural identification with Italy to this:

> My father felt that he didn't owe Italy any allegiance. So he didn't owe the country, because the country didn't give him anything because my father grew up in the war. He was a war baby, right, and so his story was always [that] there was nothing there. ... But again, my father really allowed himself to become assimilated into my mother's culture. My father went to church with us, even though he didn't speak Afrikaans, but he could understand it.

This resulted in Lara's mother's Afrikaans culture becoming more dominant, affecting the children and their connection to Italian culture.

In the case of Susanna, she experienced an ambivalent relationship with Italy which mirrored her own parents' experiences of exclusion as immigrants to South Africa after World War II during the apartheid years,

I think they were into … I think they had very complicated relationship with their Italian-ness …[laughing] which now they really want to embrace. … But I think at that stage they were scared because it was not a free society. They just felt […] ja, just to be, pretend to be as English as possible.

When a breakdown of the family unit took place, this also affected the children's relationship with Italy, as in the case of Beatrice, whose parents divorced when she was young:

> The abusive dysfunctional childhood that caused the eradication of my identity. I think that if that was intact, it would have held, that would have been the glue that held and then it would have had a lot more meaning. […] because Italian was such a secondary thing in my life, it wasn't, yes, instilled and it wasn't so deep in my core.

In establishing the central role of families in the stories of our participants, we noticed that two specific cultural markers were foregrounded, namely language and food.

Language

Both second- and third-generation participants underscored the role of their grandparents in exposing them to the Italian language. Even though many of the participants were not fluent in Italian, most of them had strong recollections of their grandparents speaking Italian to them when they were growing up: "*I have many friends of Italian descent who only spoke [Italian], or whose grandparents were with them permanently and that's how they picked up Italian*" (Angelo). This was also Alberto's experience: "*We do speak Italian at home, specifically with my nonni [grandparents] more than anyone else. They've really been the biggest push for me speaking Italian.*" Similarly, Marcelle remembered: "*Nonna spoke Italian to me, my nonno spoke Italian.*"

While there was "exposure" to the Italian language, this did not necessarily translate into language proficiency. In order to obtain this, participants had to pursue studying Italian in a more structured environment, as Antonio explained:

> And obviously, you know, you pick up a few words here and there from what they would say. But obviously it's a completely different structure so my sister and I are both decided to enrol at the Dante Alighieri at the beginning of last year, I think.

Specific language strategies were also described by our participants reflecting the challenges experienced by Italian migrants in South African society.

South Africa is a country with a historically fraught and complex linguistic landscape, with 11 official languages, of which only English is used as the lingua franca today. During the apartheid years, when many of the second-generation participants were children, the two official languages were English and Afrikaans.

Several second-generation participants had parents who could not speak English properly and this led them to speak Italian at home, as Nino explained: *"At that time my parents still didn't know English properly. So me and my brother were raised as Italian being our first language."* For most of the original immigrants, speaking English was definitely a challenge, as Gabriella described: *"My mum actually has never, in the many years she's been here ... well, she's tried to learn English, but she still has that very Italian accent and she doesn't really understand a lot."*

Being married to an English-speaking partner also led to children being brought up speaking primarily English, as Matteo recounts: *"So unfortunately, you see, because you go home and then your wife speaks English ... I have made a big mistake in my life and it's just much easier to speak English."* This phenomenon has been discussed in the work of Alba et al. (2020), who argue that mixed-language marriages often result in a specific language being spoken at home, which consequently has an impact on the third generation. The challenge of bringing up a child in a mixed linguistic environment was described by Donatella: *"I try and speak Italian to him [her son] and then he answers me in English. I change to English ... he keeps telling me that he comes from ... he keeps telling everyone that he comes from my tummy and from Italy."*

In many instances it seems as if Italian parents spoke Italian to their eldest child, but when these children encountered linguistic challenges upon entering the school system, the parents switched to speaking English (and then did so almost from the start with the younger children). This was the case for Tullio: *"and then, and then I went to school. My mother and my father got a smack on their hands and they said please start ... changing the languages. You need to speak English."* A similar scenario was described by Lilla: *"So my brother, [...] they tried to speak to him but they found that when he went to school it was very hard for him. He mixed up words, you know, code switching and what not."* This tendency shows that Italian migrant families were forced to foreground English so as to ensure academic success and also perhaps to address parents' own insecurities with English. In this regard, Marcelle recalled: *"My father spoke English to me because he said he wanted me to speak English properly. It was his fixation"* (Marcelle). Nesteruk (2010) and Nesteruk et al. (2009) have similarly reported that in the United States, for many immigrant parents, being able to master English is seen as an important tool to ensure academic and eventual professional success. Furthermore, Alba et al. (2002) point out a widespread belief that full linguistic assimilation is necessary to attain opportunities for socio-economic mobility.

This preference for English may also be ascribed to some of the prejudices experienced by the original Italian immigrants in apartheid South Africa, as described by Sandra, who said that her parents *"made a conscious decision and it was because of apartheid"*. She explained: *"my mom and dad felt discriminated against for being immigrants and they just didn't want us to live with that, they wanted us to fit in as much as possible and speak English and so we just had English."*

In many cases, Italian families also engage in language and code switching (Clyne, 2000), as Nadia remembered: *"for my father especially and to this day, we sometimes, we interchange between English and Italian."* Interestingly, there was not much evidence of the use of regional dialects in the family context, in contrast with other research on the Italian diaspora (see, for example, Finocchiaro, 2004; Giampapa, 2004). In research on Australians of Italian descent, it was found that dialect is perceived as the language of family and relatives, especially in relation to older family members (Benatti & Tarantini, 2018). However, with two exceptions, it did not emerge as a prominent linguistic tendency in our study. Nadia stated that in her family home, speaking dialect was deemed acceptable: *"It's a language all on its own and we are very proud of it. In my house it is not considered* maleducato *(rude) to speak dialect."* The use of dialect by grandparents was also something Matteo recalled: *"but my grandparents spoke dialects to us. ... I understand it all. And when we socialize in the village when I go back every year, I am able to converse in dialect."* However, it may well be that if we had interviewed the original immigrants, we might have encountered different linguistic phenomena. This may also have been because the majority of marriages reported by our participants were either between an Italian and a non-Italian, or between two Italians with different regional backgrounds, so there was no common dialect in the family.

Generally, our participants' Italian language competence varied from very fluent to rudimentary, mostly reflecting the process of language transmission described by Nesteruk (2010). Consequently, the second-generation participants tended to be more fluent than those from the third generation, although several participants admitted that they were better at speaking than at writing Italian – *"Why, my spelling is so bad, really my spelling is atrocious"* (Beatrice) and *"We could speak it very well if you hear it but to read and write, we hadn't really done that"* (Nino). However, a loss of Italian competence was evident once participants entered the school system and encountered more English-speaking peers: *"Then my mother started with the changes of the language and to this day, it's now predominantly English and, and the Italian is by the by"* (Tullio). Therefore, as children moved from their Italian nuclear family into the larger South African society, the pressure to speak the dominant English language seemed to prevail, as described earlier.

One crucial aspect which emerged, even in those who could not speak Italian, was a general eagerness to learn the language and, in some cases, a sense of regret at not having learnt it as a child:

I was thinking of perhaps going to Dante Alighieri to do an advanced course in Italian, because remember I never got to read it. I mean I never got to write it ... But speaking is not a problem [...] and I say, well, it's not too late, you can go to the Dante Alighieri if you want to but don't lose that little bit of heritage.

(Diego)

Laura also explained how she saw learning Italian as a way to connect with her Italian father and to reconnect to her Italian identity: "*It is very embarrassing going to Italy and you have an Italian passport and an Italian name and you can't understand, and I wanted to get to know my father in that way as well.*" This is in line with Tannenbaum and Howie's (2002) view that an attachment to one's family of origin is a precursor for language maintenance in migrant families.

Language competency is not only about a phenomenological description of the second and third generations' experiences, but it also has relevance for one's sense of identity. This brings us to the important question of whether one needs to speak Italian in order to feel "Italian" or "be Italian", pointing to the connection between language and ethnic identity which has been highlighted in the literature, for example, by Benatti and Tarantini (2018).

Nino expressed the belief that language and identity are strongly connected: "*I believe your identity is rooted in the way you act ... this is why I say the identity part has also to do with language.*" Nino was fluent in Italian, having always been spoken to in Italian at home by his parents. For those participants who were not fluent in Italian, learning Italian was a way to reconnect with their Italian identity: "*I got annoyed because I wanted to know where I came from, I went and I learned it. In high school I took it as a subject and then I took it right up to honours at university*" (Sandra). It was their own personal choice, as in the case of Fabrizio, whose "*parents didn't force [him] to do anything, [he] just wanted to study Italian*".

Lara lamented that not speaking Italian influenced her sense of Italian identity: "*I think if I had [...] been brought up speaking Italian, I would have much more of a sense of Italianness.*" Furthermore, she felt that not speaking the language was a source of embarrassment, especially given that (by coincidence) all our participants held both South African and Italian citizenship: "*so that's one of the reasons why I learned Italian because I am, like, I can't have this passport. And then I don't know how to ask someone, like, where the bathroom is. It's not okay.*"

In Theodore's case, he felt that not being fluent in Italian distinguished him from "real" Italians, making him different:

I found from other Italians that Italians who speak Italian and Italians who don't, the Italians who speak Italian think of the Italians who don't as non-Italian. ... there is only the language barrier but, [...] like I said,

I fight to be a part of it, so I want to be and really if I could I would raise my children to speak Italian. But I would have to learn Italian first. ... My godmother was saying that we will only ever be stranieri, ... As if they are more Italian than we are but it is something that sticks in my throat, and I feel ... I am upset that we don't have that language or that I wasn't raised in it.

Among those participants who do not speak Italian, there was a sense that language fluency was not the only thing that defined their sense of *italianità*. Angelo argued that *"being Italian is more than just the language"*. This view was supported by Barbara's remark that *"I am not saying you have to speak the language to be Italian"*. Such comments are similar to the findings of Sala (2017), who found that in Australia, second-generation participants did not think that being unable to speak the language took away from their sense of their Italian identity. In our sample, even though language competency in Italian did not seem to have a direct influence on the sense of participants' *italianità*, across the board, irrespective of whether participants were making an effort to master the language, Italian was deemed an important feature. Some of those who did not speak it expressed a desire to learn it, and none disregarded Italian as having no place in their lives.

"When it comes to the food, it's all Italian": the relation of food to identity

Many participants highlighted the significant role that food played in their families' daily lives, as well as in their sense of identity. Whilst this may seem to refer to a stereotype of Italian culture, it was in fact a central aspect of the second and third generations' sense of *italianità*. At the core of these experiences lies the tendency to view food as a "particular type of symbolic resource which may be used by migrants in processes of transition" (Greco Morasso & Zittoun, 2014, p. 31), whilst also leading to practices of commensality and conviviality (Greco Morasso & Zittoun, 2014). These authors argue that food and eating are often a way to socialize children in a family to a specific culture. They stress the nostalgic character inherent in food in migrant families, which has also been described by Locher et al. (2005). This means that food "is often linked to memories and used to maintain ethnic identity" (Greco Morasso & Zittoun, 2014, p. 29). The nostalgic connotation of food identified by Locher at al. (2005) suggests how eating certain foods may help support one's sense of cultural identity and maintain a sense of self-continuity following the disruption brought about by migration. One may therefore see nostalgic foods as a way to identify with a certain time in one's family history.

Participants described how food touched on many aspects of their familial experiences. In some instances, it was about who cooked the food. Marina said that because of her *"parents and grandparents, we have learned all the traditions of cooking and the traditional meals"*. Charles underlined the role of his grandparents: "*My grandfather was very old when he came here, compara-tively ... And he was making [...] prosciutto, salsiccia, and brewing grappa.*" Food also provided an opportunity for families to come together, as Gabriella described: "*We used to, when my grandparents here were still alive. We have a massive family. So when they were here, it was ... to get everyone together. We used to have these big lunches on a Sunday.*" Get-togethers also played a role in reinforcing one's Italian identity, as Lilla mentioned: "*Ah you know I feel more Italian ... like we do family lunches and we eat specific food.*"

Sharing meals also provided participants with opportunities to be exposed to the Italian language, as Antonio recalls:

> And we, ja, we'd go see them once a week, once every two weeks as a family, every Sunday, or every second Sunday we'd all come together for family; my nonna would always cook. And obviously, you know, you pick up a few words here and there from what they would say.

This was also Carla's experience:

> So you have a little family gathering every Sunday and obviously my gran cooks nice food, so it's mainly the food side of things. I have my favourite Italian dishes and that sort of thing, and then, ... I don't know, my family ... they speak Italian around me when I'm there.

The eating of certain foods was also closely linked to specific rituals, mostly religious, associated with Christmas and Easter, which have already been described earlier in this chapter, and which was seen as an important part of family life: "*at Christmas [...] we will always have ... Panettone and things. Mostly it would just be like the standard food that [you] would have, you know, Easter there will be a Colomba and you still have a Pandoro*" (Barbara).

These experiences were often juxtaposed with the local or "English" foods. Barbara recounted:

> I identify a lot with the food and that [is] because that's what I got brought up eating, I remember. Actually chicken hasn't been a part of our diet growing up and then I remember going to friends' houses when I was younger and they would serve us fish fingers or some weird chicken thing. ...And then they would come to my house and ... my mom would be serving tongue and I don't know what, you know. So, and then my Nonno was an amazing cook. My mom is as well, actually.

This difference resulted in a sense of pride in the superiority of Italian cooking and ways of sharing meals, as Charles indicated:

So, there is a little thing that will really get on my nerves, when […] in the English food culture […] you have to wait for everyone to start eating and it has to be a slow process to get to the table and you have to have ten drinks and… in our culture the food is the centre and when the pasta is ready you sit and you eat it.

This difference was felt particularly in instances when a participant's partner was not Italian. Matteo was quite adamant in this respect:

Then obviously all our eating habits are Italian, completely, even now my wife is not Italian, but at my house, the eating is all Italian, my children are 11 and 14 and already then they … when it comes to the food, it's all Italian.

Conclusion

Our participants' stories clearly demonstrate that their family of origin, and especially grandparents, played a vital role in the transmission and fostering of their sense of *italianità*. This was evident from the varied and mostly close family relationships that the participants described. The family of origin appears to be an intimate space where cultural markers such as language and food are cultivated, playing an important role in the process of cultural transmission.

References

Alba, R., Logan, J., Lutz, A., & Stults, B. (2002). Only English by the third generation? Loss and preservation of the mother tongue among the grandchildren of contemporary immigrants. *Demography, 39*(3), 467–484. https://doi.org/10.1353/dem.2002.0023

Benatti, R., & Tarantini, A. T. (2018). Dialects among young Italian-Australians: A shift in attitude and perception. *Studia Anglica Posnaniensia, 52*(4), 467–483. https://doi.org/10.1515/stap-2017-0021

Clyne, M. (2000). Constraints on code-switching: How universal are they? In L. Wei (Ed.), *The bilingualism reader* (pp. 257–280). Routledge.

Di Nicola, V. (1997). *A stranger in the family: Culture, families, and therapy.* Norton.

Falicov, C. J. (1995). Training to think culturally: A multidimensional comparative framework. *Family Process, 34*(4), 373–388. https://doi.org/10.1111/j.1545-5300.1995.00373.x

Falicov, C. J. (2007). Working with transnational immigrants: Expanding meanings of family, community, and culture. *Family Process, 46*(2), 157–171. https://doi.org/10.1111/j.1545-5300.2007.00201.x

Falicov, C. J. (2009). Religion and spiritual traditions in immigrant families: Significance for Latino health and mental health. In F. Walsh (Ed.), *Spiritual resources in family therapy* (pp. 156–173). New York: Guilford Press.

Finocchiaro, D. C. M. (2004). *Language maintenance shift of a three generation Italian family in three migration countries: An international comparative study* [Doctoral dissertation, University of Melbourne]. https://minerva-access.unimelb.edu.au/handle/11343/39049

Giampapa, F. (2004). *Italian Canadian youth and the negotiation of identities: The discourse on italianità, language and the spaces of identity* [PhD dissertation, University of Toronto]. https://tspace.library.utoronto.ca/handle/1807/121302

Greco Morasso, S., & Zittoun, T. (2014). The trajectory of food as a symbolic resource for international migrants. *Outlines – Critical Practice Studies,15*(1), 28–48. https://doi.org/10.7146/ocps.v15i1.15828

Locher, J. L., Yoels, W. C., Maurer, D., & Van Ells, J. (2005). Comfort foods: An exploratory journey into the social and emotional significance of food. *Food and Foodways, 13*(4), 273–297. https://doi.org/10.1080/07409710500334509

Marchetti-Mercer, M. C. (2006). New meanings of "home" in South Africa. *Acta Academica, 38*(2), 191–218.

McGoldrick, M., Giordano, J., & Garcia-Preto, N. (Eds.). (2005). *Ethnicity and family therapy*. Guilford Press.

McGoldrick, M., Pearce, J. K., & Giordano, J. (Eds.). (1982). *Ethnicity and family therapy*. Guilford Press.

Nesteruk, O. (2010). Heritage language maintenance and loss among the children of Eastern European immigrants in the USA. *Journal of Multilingual and Multicultural Development, 31*(3), 271–286. https://doi.org/10.1080/01434630903582722

Nesteruk, O., Marks, L., & Garrison, M. E. B. (2009). Immigrant parents' concerns regarding their children's education in the United States. *Family and Consumer Sciences Research Journal, 37*(4), 422–441. https://doi.org/10.1177/1077727X08330671

Papadopoulos, R. K. (2002). Refugees, home and trauma. In R. K. Papadopoulos (Ed.), *Therapeutic care for refugees: No place like home* (pp. 9–39). Karnac Books.

Sala, E. (2017). *The Italian-ness is in the family: A critical evaluation of the role of family in constructions of ethnicity and connections to homeland among two cohorts of second generation Italian-Australians* [Doctoral dissertation, PhD Thesis, University of Western Australia]. https://api.research-repository.uwa.edu.au/ws/portalfiles/portal/ 20507794/THESIS_DOCTOR_OF_PHILOSOPHY_SAL A_Emanuela_2017.pdf

Sala, E., & Baldassar, L. (2017). "I don't do much in the community as an Italian, but in my family I do": A critique of symbolic ethnicity through a longitudinal study of second-generation Italian Australians. *Journal of Anthropological Research, 73*(4), 557–583. https://doi.org/10.1086/694683

Tannenbaum, M., & Howie, P. (2002). The association between language maintenance and family relations: Chinese immigrant children in Australia. *Journal of Multilingual and Multicultural Development, 23*(5), 408–424. https://doi.org/10.1080/01434630208666477

Walsh, F. (2009). Religion, spirituality, and the family: Multifaith perspectives. In F. Walsh (Ed.), *Spiritual resources in family therapy* (pp. 3–30). Guilford Press.

6 "I find it unique and I am proud to be Italian"

The relationship with Italy and the larger Italian community in South Africa

Introduction

The ability to construct and maintain a transnational identity in migrant communities has grown considerably in recent years, mainly as a result of increased possibilities for material and virtual exchanges between the country of origin and the destination country (Vertovec, 2009). In this chapter, we explore the relationship of second- and third-generation Italians in South Africa with Italy in respect of their identity and their sense of pride in their Italian heritage. We focus specifically on some aspects of Italian popular culture that we identified as important markers of participants' sense of identity. We also describe their participation in current Italian political affairs and in the larger Italian community in South Africa.

Ethnic identity and *italianità*

In our interviews, we investigated in depth our participants' understanding of national identity in the highly politicized context of South African society, with its fraught history and multicultural character.

All our participants held both South African and Italian citizenship (although this was not a criterion for inclusion) and described a complex relationship with their identity. We observed three main trends. Firstly, a large majority of the participants (both in the second and third generations) foregrounded their Italian roots as their primary identity marker. For example, Dario explained that he is *"Italian growing up in South Africa"*, and Tullio said: *"So if someone asks me, I will say I am Italian."* Marcelle stated: *"I am Italian ... That's how I identify [...] I don't feel South African."* Susanna was slightly less adamant: *"But I always ... I do identify with Italy, I will say I have Italian blood."*

Secondly, others described a form of dual identity. Charles said: *"I have come to terms with the fact that my identity is hybridized, I will never be like them [Italians]."* Matteo explained this in a more nuanced way: *"My situation is I am very proud of my Italian heritage but I am born in South Africa. So I always describe myself as an Italian-South African where South Africa is the noun and Italian is the adjective."*

DOI: 10.4324/9781003266884-6

Thirdly, there were also a couple of instances where the South African identity was foregrounded, as in the case of Lara, who described herself *"as a South African with Italian family"*, and Ignazio, who stated: *"I am South African, but my roots are very deep in Italy."* Lara and Ignazio came from families where their Italian parent or grandparent had married a local Afrikaans-speaking South African. Barbara also emphasized her South African roots (while acknowledging that possibly an early break-up in her family of origin limited her exposure to both her Italian parents), *"I am proudly South African, I do love South Africa, but I do say I have got an Italian background"*.

When asked about what made them feel "Italian" and what they most identified in terms of Italy, none of them mentioned that they had an Italian passport. This material symbol of nationality appeared to be taken for granted as a consequence of their heritage.

Some participants commented on a sense of Italian-ness being linked to what might be a stereotyped notion of "Italian" physical appearance; for example, Charles mentioned that he looked *"different from the average Italian"* because he is tall and has blond hair, but noted that eating and cooking certain foods contributed to a sense of being Italian. Other markers mentioned were the way people decorate their homes: *"when you walk into my house it definitely doesn't look like a South African home"* (Marcelle). Demeanour was also perceived to differentiate our participants from their South African peers: *"Like the way they [Italians] carry themselves, I think I carry myself in the same way"* (Angelo). The latter observation suggests that at times participants felt that being "Italian" potentially made them stand out from other white South Africans – *"when you tell them you are Italian they will see it in a good light"* (Antonio). Carla recalled: *"When I was younger, I used to boast that I'm Italian."* Lilla was aware that Italians may use their Italian-ness to construct themselves as different; in other words, they are not necessarily different but they "use" their Italian-ness to be perceived as different: *"A lot of Italians here love to be playing Italian. So like my generation, they always use it as a unique card, you know."*

Sense of pride in Italian heritage

We observed an overwhelming sense of pride in having an Italian heritage, across all participants. For the second-generation participants, in some cases, their sense of pride was directly linked to Italy's international achievements in terms of art and culture. It was also related to the beauty of the country, as well as other contributions by Italy in the global arena, for example, in fashion and design. The sense of pride evident in the third-generation participants was particularly intriguing, given that, in many instances, their connection to Italy was only through one Italian grandparent, as in the case of Ignazio and Theodore.

Generally, there was pride in cultural aspects associated with Italy, which often included traditional foods, as Barbara mentioned:

> *I think I am also like very proud of ... if someone is speaking about something Italian or, or when people are speaking about food, I am just very proud and privileged [...] such amazing things and such amazing culture and that like it's ... I think it is fantastic. I think I have been very lucky. [...] Italy has so much culture, you know, it is very rich in arts and food and all of those things and that I think I appreciate.*

In some ways, this sense of pride seemed to justify a desire to belong: if being Italian means being associated with so many internationally recognized artistic and cultural achievements, then there is a great value in being Italian, a value that must be preserved and cultivated. Angelo, for example, emphasized the uniqueness of Italy: "*I think with Italy it's a very unique culture, for lack of a better word.*" Laura saw a link between being Italian and being part of this Italian heritage: "*and everyone says ah this and that about Italy, but at the end of the day I am proud of my heritage. And I think also because the Italian culture is full of pride and history, you understand what it means to be Italian.*" Matteo shared the same sentiment:

> *I am very proud of my Italian heritage. I am very proud of being of Italian descent, very proud of being an Italian South African, because there's so much about Italy and the Italians that one can be proud of ... First of all, if you look at the beauty of the country; for example, if you look at the intelligence of the people, if you look at the leadership role that Italy plays in so many aspects of life, whether it's Ferrari, whether it's fashion, architecture ... so proud of the fact that 60 or 70% of the treasures of the world are in Italy.*

Lara linked her sense of pride of being Italian with something that transcended her individual experience: "*I think it's that connection to something that is sort of more timeless than our history. It's that sense of history maybe.*"

These feelings of pride may be seen as a kind of "ethnic pride" which has been associated with a positive attitude towards one's own ethnic origins and identity (Pasupathi et al., 2012). This is also a common trait in other Italian diasporas, as investigated, for example, by Alessandria et al. (2016) in the United States. However, unlike what emerged in Alessandria et al.'s (2016) study, the pride of the second and third generations in South Africa is not based on the achievements and successes of fellow Italian-South Africans, used as reference points, but rather on the Italian culture, history, and traditions in the country of origin. In countries such as the United States, the numbers of Italian immigrants were much higher, and many people of Italian descent have been very successful in the political, business, and entertainment fields.

The same is not true in South Africa, where immigrant numbers from Italy were lower, and the early history of Italian immigration is less well known (although there have been some notable figures, as discussed in Chapter 4). In fact, none of our participants mentioned any Italian-South African public figure who made them proud to be of Italian origin. This may be because in South Africa a uniquely "Italian-South African culture" has not developed: there is no established Italian-South African literature, nor a distinctive Italian-South African cuisine. Given the more recent history of the Italian migration to South Africa and the lower numbers when compared to other countries, Italians in South Africa do not have many autochthonous points of reference to which they can look up. Therefore, they are more likely to find in Italy itself a reference point from which their sense of pride emanates.

Linking up with Italian everyday life: RAI Italia, sport, and music

In exploring our participants' relationship with Italy, we also looked at their involvement with selected aspects of Italian everyday life, as well as their interest in Italian current affairs.

Exposure to Italian daily life and events has certainly increased in recent decades thanks to RAI (the national broadcasting corporation). Images of Italy are now readily available to Italians living abroad on a daily basis. RAI International (which has changed its name to RAI Italia), was created in 1995, during the Berlusconi era. It has a strong commercial and nationalistic orientation, aimed not so much at rendering a public service as at spreading (fairly stereotypical) images of Italy, with programmes on sports, cooking, music, game shows, and Catholicism (Ardizzoni, 2016). A similar assessment of the corporation was reported by Hayward (2008), who also recognized the dual nature of RAI International when it was first created: it was driven by the demands of the global media market on the one hand, and by a more nationalistic agenda on the other.

We observed in our participants' responses that RAI Italia is particularly important for Italian immigrants living in South Africa who wish to maintain a connection with Italian popular culture. Participants recounted that when they were growing up, the television in their homes was permanently tuned to RAI International. It seems to have become an almost permanent guest, always in the background, mostly in the house of their grandparents and/or parents. For example, Alberto recalled that "*in terms of Italian TV, growing up RAI was always on TV. So you know it was always watching and all those type of stuff*". Carla shared that she still watches RAI, "*when I go to my gran's house*". Lilla remembered: "*So my grandmother, my mom, I know, used to always watch RAI.*" Gabriella's experience also confirmed the ever-present conscious or subliminal awareness of RAI in the home:

[E]very day when you walk into my house, the RAI is on in the back-ground. Even though no one's watching it, it's there. So I'm forced to watch it [chuckles], and obviously all the shows on the RAI, I know about and watch. And my mum loves watching Italian movies. So, ja, basically all the time ... I do actually [watch RAI] more than South African news, which is bad because I know nothing about what's happening here, but I know everything that's happening there [chuckles]. So, ja, it's always on. So you listen to it while you're doing your daily things.

We can therefore see that RAI is not only ever-present in Italian immigrant homes, but it is also strongly associated with the family of origin.

In some instances, it became a way in which different generations could connect. Nadia described watching the popular soap opera "Posto al Sole" in order to spend time with her father: "*and me and my father when I am with my dad – my mother doesn't watch it, so we go to the TV upstairs and it is our thing; we lie on the bed and we watch it.*" Italian television is thus often not watched alone as a private and individual event. Furthermore, interest in RAI does not derive from a personal quest for an Italian identity. Instead, it becomes a fixed and central object inside the home of one's parents and/or grandparents, creating a link between the family and Italy.

Soccer and sports in general were often mentioned as something watched on Italian television. Tullio explained: "*Yes, I like watching the Italian sports, I like watching, the Italians are very good at fencing and ...*" Interest in Italian sport is certainly one of the main features of Italian life that was shared among the participants. Not surprisingly, soccer is the most prominent among the sports mentioned, not only in relation to the Azzurri national team, but also to various clubs. Support for a favourite club is usually handed down in the context of the family – Donatella happily shared that "*[y]es, yes, my team is [laughing] Lazio but the only reason why my team is Lazio is because it was my father's team*". Barbara recounted: "*Yes – Italy – I will definitely support in the World Cup. ... I am not the biggest sports fan or anything like that, so, I know my dad and my brother support Torino.*" Nadia clearly linked her support for a particular soccer team with her origins: "*I actually have it tattooed on my pulse. So that I never forget where I am and who I am from.*" Silvio also connected his sport preferences to his broader Italian origins:

Of course it was you are supporting Italy. I don't know how that was engrained but you ... it was taught from then, that is who you support and if it's motorbikes, Ducati or Aprilia used to be, then Ducati got in and then it was Ducati. So that was ... and then my uncle, he was an avid Formula One fan and a motor GP fan and ... that's where I would spend my Sundays as well, just watching that and then understanding, so the Ferrari connection is big.

There seems to be limited research on the importance of sport as a cultural aggregator for Italians abroad. An exception is the work of Ricatti and Klugman (2013), who observed that, as in the second and third generations in our study

> [t]he soccer teams and culture that Italian migrants created in Australia, [...] reaffirmed and strengthened their connections to their homeland. And this created an avenue for their sons and daughters who arrived in Australia as children, or were born in Australia, to experience, negotiate with and feel connected to their Italian heritage.

(p. 473)

When we explored participants' music preferences, we saw more eclectic individual taste which was not linked to the family of origin. The Italian music that the second- and third-generation participants listened to was also influenced by current trends, and is probably different from the preferences of their parents or grandparents. For example, Angelo shared the following: *"So I listen to Marco Mengoni and Maneskin and that kind ... a few of those guys. I do listen to a lot more Italian music now as well."* Barbara recalled that when she was younger, she *"used to love Eros Ramazzotti"*, evidently referring to the period in which Eros Ramazzotti was a very popular singer after he won the Sanremo song festival in 1984. Laura shared a similar experience: *"I do like some Italian music as well. Laura Pausini and Eros Ramazzotti."*

Significantly, to be appreciated, sports and music do not require language competence in Italian, which is probably one reason they are so popular amongst these descendants of the original immigrants. The second and third generations can easily connect to Italy in this way, without any language barrier. Watching RAI television, the situation is slightly different. As we have observed, RAI is often a constant background presence in parents' and grandparents' homes: it is not always listened to actively by members of the second and third generations. In fact, the content of programmes often has to be translated for them, as Carla admitted: *"Then they have to always tell me what's happening because I don't understand."* The language barrier may also prevent consumption of other cultural goods, such as Italian books and newspapers, which were seldom mentioned among the experiences of our participants.

Voting in the Italian election

At the end of 2001, the Italian parliament approved new legislation which gives Italians living abroad the right to vote in Italian national elections and to be represented by their own members in the Italian parliament. The new law has important consequences for Italians living abroad, as it includes them in the larger political process and also recognizes holders of Italian passports as transnational citizens of Italy (see Aliano, 2010; Battiston & Mascitelli, 2008). It also potentially addressed Italian migrants' sense of belonging to Italy.

Lähdesmäki et al. (2016) and Yuval-Davis (2006) distinguish between psychological and political belonging. Psychological belonging involves emotional attachment related to feeling at home and feeling safe, while political belonging involves participation in a political community, including "citizenship, entitlement, and status" (Lähdesmäki et al., 2016, p. 19). Citizenship, which all our participants held in the form of an Italian passport, comes with a sense of entitlement, which is also linked to participation in a political system, and specifically to the right to vote. Citizenship can be seen as a manifestation of belonging, as it designates a formal, public, and imagined membership into a nation (Antonsich, 2010; Bonnet, 2021; Yuval-Davis, 2006).

However, despite the potential opportunity to participate in Italian political life, when we asked participants about their understanding of and involvement in Italian politics, their responses reflected a noticeable lack of engagement with these processes. Most participants admitted that as an "outsider" it is very difficult to understand the Italian political system. Language was identified as a major barrier, for example, by Donatella: *"And all of that, however, it is very difficult to understand, really, I mean, I don't understand."* This lack of linguistic understanding was reflected in most participants' unease with the opportunity to vote. Some had voted in elections but complained that they found the system complicated and did not really know for whom to vote. They often ended up asking family members for advice, as in Gabriella's case:

> The ballot forms [came] in the post, and it had my name on it. So I'm pretty sure I voted. I just don't remember, and my parents told me who to vote for [chuckles] because I don't follow politics, if that makes sense. So, ja, I remember getting it; I'm sure I did; I just don't remember.

Diego shared a similar experience, even though he asked family members in Italy for information:

> I thought well if you can't give me guidance and you live there then I am much more in the dark. ... you can Google and you can [...] try and get as much information as to what are the policies and what does that party believe and its .... You are doing it from afar. ... I did once. Because that came from the Consolato and with years to come, you know, I have ... I don't know enough about the ... who actually to vote for ... speaking to my cousins, in Italy I mean, they just said, look, it's a bit of a mess.

Tullio echoes this sentiment: *"I would say to my mother which party are you voting for and then I will ask her, which family party ... they, in Italy, what vote to look for, and then they will say, you know"*. There were, however, two exceptions, Nadia and Matteo, who were quite well-versed in politics in general and had a keen interest in what was happening in the Italian political system: *"I do. I follow it very closely. I vote"* (Nadia).

Third-generation participants expressed even more difficulties associated with voting in the Italian elections. Both the language barrier and the difficulty of understanding the Italian political system and staying up to date on what is happening in Italy seemed to be the main deterrents to their voting. Carla expresses her confusion as follows: *"I've seen [...]my gran would turn over to the news, and they'd be like this is what's happening, this is the prime minister, it's new or whatever, but I don't know any."* Even when there is some interest in Italian current affairs, choosing whom to vote for is still a difficult exercise, as Silvio recounted:

> *Whenever I do go back to Italy, I do catch up quickly on what has been happening, what's progressed, but I think it's more on the political side. I think if I look at the way it's progressed, there has been a lot of changes, whereas back in 2005, there was a lot more xenophobia, so especially with the West Africans coming in ... Well, the thing is I read up about the profiles and then you see, okay, that one is supporting Africa but you are not sure if you should be and who these parties are but it's good to read up, I have never voted in that way.*

The same challenges were expressed even by some of those who did vote, suggesting a sense of dissatisfaction, as Alberto reported: *"So last year was the first year that I voted. I know, wow. It wasn't my favourite thing. I didn't really vote for who I wanted to but I think ..."* Laura saw voting as a right that needs to be exercised, as an Italian passport holder. However, this did not dispel the difficulties expressed by others:

> *So I vote there, [...] I feel like if you have the privilege of having dual nationality, you need to have a voice too. [...] I think it's largely because people don't understand what they are voting for, and [...] the politics are quite complex.*

Therefore, while the opportunity to take part in the Italian system may potentially have increased the sense of political belonging of those Italians living abroad (see Battiston & Mascitelli, 2008), it seems that there are several barriers that make full political participation difficult.

Involvement in the larger Italian community in South Africa

Associations and clubs are entities where migrant communities may reproduce the home country culture and create a sense of home and belonging. They provide a safe context where one's transnational identity may be negotiated and performed. Falicov (2007) has highlighted the importance of ethnic community networks in immigrants' lives. This may also contribute to immigrants' mental health (Vega et al., 1991). Ainslie's (1998) work on the cultural mourning of migrants highlights the importance of these communal sites to connect with compatriots in order to allay feelings of loneliness and the alienation that immigrants might experience in the destination country. This would have been the case for first-generation Italians. In the Italian community in South Africa, there are a number of associations, many linked to regional origins. However, we noticed in our research that members of the second and third generations spoke more about their participation in the Italian community at large than about membership in regional or local Italian associations. We would therefore argue that our participants used Italian associations as a way to negotiate their "Italian" ethnicity at a collective level, rather than at a regional one, as was possibly the case with their forebears.

Sometimes involvement in the larger community also derives from the family of origin:

> *Also, yes, we are very much involved in the Italian community because of our parents and grandparents. ... We have learned all the traditions of cooking and the traditional meals the way we have lunch [...] yes, I try my best and we do go to the Italian Club.*
>
> (Marina)

> *We did do the odd event at the Italian Club where we either attended or I have been, one of my aunts got married there.*
>
> (Laura)

The association most frequented by the third-generation participants was the Giovani Italo-Sudafricani, which Donatella described as follows: "*We were trying to bring Italian culture to the South African youngsters and make them more Italian and make them proud of Italy.*" Angelo commented on being part of the Association: "*It's just a totally different vibe, it's more natural.*" Carla shared that her experience of being involved in the Italian community was an "*eye opener*":

> *I actually got a bursary from them, so I've been involved now with the Italian community, which is actually ... it's an eye opener for me*

and I am actually really enjoying it, and I have also joined the Youth Committee there now.

Alberto explained in detail how the Association of the Giovani Italo-Sudafricani constitutes a way for younger generations to negotiate their Italian identity in South Africa, creating transnational subjects even when their Italian affiliation is simply constituted by a "blood link":

> *What's been quite nice is we've been able to socialize with a much greater group of people and what's really created some sort of notion for me is that regardless whether someone's grown up with a lot of "Italianesque" things in their life or whether they haven't, if they've got that heritage or they've got that surname it's something that they look forward to or they want to assimilate with in some form or manner and that's what I've really enjoyed from the Giovani and I think that's something how we've all come together. And I've actually made some really good friends in this [Association] in the last three years.*

Participating in the activities of an Italian association therefore becomes a way to affirm one's own Italian belonging, however "mediated" and South Africanized it may be. It becomes a way of being or feeling Italian in South Africa, without necessarily requiring linguistic competence or in-depth knowledge of Italian culture. Antonio reflected on this: "You know, I've got a passion for the country. So, ja, and I also think it just gave me a bit of a sense of belonging." This may reflect the phenomenon of an intra-diaspora mentioned by Lee (2011), as discussed in Chapter 3, which reveals that many second-generation immigrants may identify more readily with those who share their experience as the children of immigrants, and in our case, mostly as the grandchildren of immigrants.

Conclusion

Although our participants grew up in a country which differed from some of their parents' or grandparents' country of birth, they seemed to experience a connection with Italy and a sense of pride in their Italian roots, linked to the beauty and cultural aspects of Italy. This connection did not necessarily translate into political participation. The connection with the local Italian community seemed to be moving away from regional connections, which were more evident in the lives of the original immigrants. There seemed to be a resurgence of participation in the third-generation Italians, who seem to have found some sense of belonging in the fairly recently constituted Giovani Italo-Sudafricani association.

References

Ainslie, R. (1998). Cultural mourning, immigration, and engagement: Vignettes from the Mexican experience. In M. M. Suárez-Orozco (Ed.), *Crossings: Mexican immigration in interdisciplinary perspectives* (pp. 285–300). Harvard University Press.

Alessandria, K. P., Kopacz, M. A., Goodkin, G., Valerio, C., & Lappi, H. (2016). Italian American ethnic identity persistence: A qualitative study. *Identity: An International Journal of Theory and Research, 16*(4), 1–17. http://doi.org/10.1080/15283488.2016.1229610

Aliano, D. (2010). Citizenship and belonging: The case of the Italian vote abroad. *Ethnic Studies Review, 33*(1), 36–60. https://doi.org/10.1525/esr.2010.33.1.36

Antonsich, M. (2010). Searching for belonging – An analytical framework. *Geography Compass, 4*(6), 644–659. https://doi.org/10.1111/j.1749-8198.2009.00317.x

Ardizzoni, M. (2016). Borderless nationalism: RAI's transnational brand. In Z. Volcic & M. Andrejevic (Eds.), *Commercial nationalism: Selling the nation and nationalizing the sell* (pp. 131–146). Palgrave Studies in Communication for Social Change. Palgrave McMillan. https://doi.org/10.1057/9781137500991_8

Battiston, S., & Mascitelli, B. (2008). Full voting rights for Italian citizens overseas: Citizenship gone global, Italianness or Italian party politics. In S. Bronitt & K. Rubenstein (Eds.), *Citizenship in a post-national world: Australia and Europe compared* (pp. 1–23). Federation Press. https://www.researchgate.net/publication/330728619_Full_Voting_Rights_for_Italian_Citizens_Overseas_Citizenship_Gone_Global_Italianness_or_Italian_Party_Politics

Bonnet, A. (2021). *Belonging and family relationships: The experiences of immigrants in Olievenhoutbosch* [Master's thesis in Community-based Counselling Psychology, University of the Witwatersrand]. https://hdl.handle.net/10539/33480

Falicov, C. J. (2007). Working with transnational immigrants: Expanding meanings of family, community, and culture. *Family Process, 46*(2), 157–171. https://doi.org/10.1111/j.1545-5300.2007.00201.x

Hayward, M. (2008). *Global Italy: Media, identity and the future of the nation-state.* [PhD dissertation, University of North Carolina at Chapel Hill Graduate School]. https://doi.org/10.17615/kzzx-1317

Lähdesmäki, T., Saresma, T., Hiltunen, K., Jäntti, S., Sääskilahti, N., Vallius, A., & Ahvenjärvi, K. (2016). Fluidity and flexibility of "belonging": Uses of the concept in contemporary research. *Acta Sociologica, 59*(3), 233–247. https://doi.org/10.1177/0001699316663309

Lee, H. (2011). Rethinking transnationalism through the second generation. *Australian Journal of Anthropology, 22*(3), 295–313. https://doi.org/10.1111/j.1757-6547.2011.00150.x

Pasupathi, M., Wainryb, C., & Twali, M. (2012). Relations between narrative construction of ethnicity-based discrimination and ethnic identity exploration and pride. *Identity: An International Journal of Theory and Research, 12*(1), 53–73. https://doi.org/10.1080/15283488.2012.632393

Ricatti, F., & Klugman, M. (2013). Connected to something: Soccer and the transnational passions, memories and communities of Sydney's Italian migrants. *The International Journal of the History of Sport, 30*(5), 469–483. https://doi.org/10.1080/09523367.2013.770735

Vega, W., Kolody, B., Valle, R., & Weir, J. (1991). Social networks, social support, and their relationship to depression among immigrant Mexican women. *Human Organization, 50*(2), 154–162. https://doi.org/10.17730/humo.50.2.p340266397214724

Vertovec, S. (2009). *Transnationalism.* Routledge.

Yuval-Davis, N. (2006). Belonging and the politics of belonging. *Patterns of Prejudice, 40*(3), 197–214. https://doi.org/10.1080/00313220600769331

7 "The point of going to Italy is the sense of belonging"

The meaning of visits to Italy

Introduction

The significance of visits to one's ancestors' land of origin to second- and third-generation Italian immigrants, as well as the "homecoming" aspect of such trips (Basu, 2004; King & Christou, 2010), has already been mentioned in Chapter 3. In her research on second-generation Italians in Australia, Baldassar (2001, 2011) describes such visits back to Italy as a kind of "pilgrimage" which forms part of the life cycle of the descendants of the original immigrants. We also regard these visits as an important part of the transnational experience of the second and third generations of Italians in South Africa.

The seed for "return" visits is often planted in childhood, when the children and grandchildren of immigrants travel to Italy with their families, typically for a summer vacation (Levitt, 2002). Wessendorf (2007) has reported that regular holidays to Italy during the summer months played a crucial role in her second-generation participants' identity formation. According to her, in many instances, such visits also shaped their desire eventually to "return" to Italy as adults, a phenomenon that she describes as "roots migration". In our research, we found that the majority of our participants were taken to Italy as children or adolescents, mostly with the specific intention of visiting remaining family members still living there. Some decided to move to Italy on a more permanent basis as adults but encountered a number of challenges, which we describe later.

The role of family roots vacations

Taking one's children or grandchildren back to one's land of origin is part of many immigrant families' transnational experiences. In this manner, ties with the country of origin are maintained and even passed on to younger generations. Based on the findings of our study, we have described such visits as "family roots vacations", borrowing from and adapting Wessendorf's (2007) term, as they usually took place in the context of the family when parents and/ or grandparents took our participants to Italy. From the original immigrants'

DOI: 10.4324/9781003266884-7

side, these visits also served as a cultural introduction of their country of origin to their descendants. This intention was clear from Donatella's words when she recalled a visit to Italy with her son:

> It is so difficult and the only way I can think of doing this, is also bringing him to Italy. Like for a month at a time and, and staying with … thank God I have got family there. And introducing them to … my cousin's kids that are his age and I get a lot of Italian friends coming to stay with me.

For the original Italian immigrants to South Africa, we needed to consider that despite a willingness to take such "family roots vacations", logistical factors may have had an impact on the frequency of trips. The high costs and long travelling time associated with flights to Italy make the journey challenging. The Euro–South African Rand exchange rate continues to pose difficulties for travel from South Africa to any European destination. These facts are in line with Horn's (2017) findings. He mentions several practical constraints that restrict migrants' visits – "migrants' socio-economic resources, time, health and mobility rights […]. In other words, a migrant needs money, time, a regular migration status and good enough health to board a plane" (Horn, 2017, p. 521).

Matteo spoke at length of how being taken by his parents to Italy on holiday as a child contributed greatly to his sense of belonging. Arguably, this kind of experience is often a powerful motivator to the second generation, as King and Christou (2010) note. They regard this "returning" to the country of origin of one's forebears as crucial to subsequent generations' search for home and belonging. Matteo followed a similar path with his own children:

> So, the point of going to Italy is the sense of belonging – to say this is where my ancestors were born and I am attached to the place because that's where I come from. … [Something] I still appreciate today is the fact that we were taken to Italy from the time we were children. And we knew exactly where we came from, which, for anybody in life, that's important to know where you come from. […] So we must never stop taking our children and our future generations to Italy, because that's where you belong and that's where the Italian community in this country have succeeded. And when I took my sons (one is 14 and one is 11) […] to the cemetery in my father's village, I was able to show them the tombstones of all their ancestors. The great, great, great, great, great grandparents. And when they came out of that cemetery, they were different people, you know, so, [a] sense of belonging [is] very important.

Many of the participants' responses reflected the joy and pleasure they experienced during those visits: "*We went for a month. And it was amazing, we just did Italy. We were like now we don't want to go to the rest of Europe, we just want to go to Italy"* (Federica); *"That was amazing, that was one of the highlights of my life"* (Ignazio).

An important objective of such visits is also to reconnect with the families of origin who still live in the country of origin. Consequently, family visits potentially function as a way of maintaining, renewing, and solidifying family ties across borders (Bryceson & Vuorela, 2002; Horn, 2017). This was reflected in a number of our participants' experiences. Nino described it as follows: *"I went obviously because all my family is there, so obviously when my mom and my dad had us, they would take us there and then the grandparents playing with us and everyone, you know, the family see ...."* This was also Marcelle's experience:

> I was about five, we went; but I mean we used to go every year to Italy. My first memory was all the aunties and cousins in Trieste ... The family, always the family. Always spending time with the mother figures in the kitchen, always watching how they [were] cooking and what they cook.

The initial connections formed during these holidays often resulted in more permanent relationships with family members back in Italy – *"We were in close contact and especially after our visit for the first time"* (Ignazio), *"I mean I am actually in contact with the younger generation of my [family] that were from my dad's side"* (Diego), and *"And so, yes, so it's more, I have a connection to my family in Italy"* (Lara).

Regular communication between visits was mostly maintained through the use of information communication technologies, as Nino described:

> Yeah. So try, I speak, I Skype my nonna. Yeah, so I've got my nonna and then my aunts, and my cousins, everybody and so I Skype them and I ask them what's going on because they want me to go back there, you know.

Nadia described her communication with her Italian family as follows:

> I am in touch with them all the time. I get a message from my cousins every single day. I speak to L[...] at least once a week, if not twice a week and it's [...] an incredibly strong bond because [vernacular] so the only way that we have our hold ... through communication and technology now is wonderful.

Social media is a popular platform, as Federica explained: *"[S]ocial media makes it a lot easier, you suddenly can find like everyone on Instagram and you can check what they are doing. And you can wish them merry Christmas and that kind of stuff."* The usefulness of social media was reiterated by Donatella: *"We have got a WhatsApp group, Facebook, every day we talk. Every day."*

The role of information communication technologies in maintaining relationships in transnational families in between physical visits has been explored at length in the literature. Different forms of technology allow a form of virtual co-presence (Baldassar, 2016a, 2016b; Marchetti-Mercer et al., 2021) during those times when physical visits are not possible. This notion of "virtual co-presence" reflects the way in which people, and, in our case, immigrants and their families left behind, can still be there for each other despite the geographical distance (Baldassar, 2016a, 2016b; Baldassar et al., 2016).

Forming relationships with Italian family members also encouraged participants to learn or improve their Italian – *"I've got cousins ... they're not exactly very proficient in English, so the Italian part is very important because that's the only way ... we can actually maintain a relationship"* (Alberto). A trip to Italy provided the impetus for Silvio to learn some Italian, *"I was more interested in it, so I try to keep the Italian going. Don't want to lose that. I want to hold the strong ties with the family."* The advantage of connection in maintaining Italian language skills was also elucidated by Lara:

> I wanted to go to Italy and I have got lots of family there; they don't speak English at all. So [the] not speaking Italian thing was an issue for me because, well, because half my family [says] I can't talk to you. So I had Italian lessons twice a week with an Italian lady in Pretoria, Signora P[...]. So she taught me the rudiments of grammar and some of the vocab and stuff and then I went to Italy to visit my family.

Those who visited regularly as children believed that those trips had cemented their Italian proficiency, as in the case of Nadia, who said her *"Italian was good because [she] used to go to Italy so often"*. These experiences resonate with the findings of Nesteruk and Marks (2009), who argue that visits to their parents' country of origin are important for younger generations in maintaining their forebears' native language, because of the need to communicate with non-English-speaking family members in the country of origin.

There was also some evidence of visits from family members living in Italy to South Africa, which likewise helped strengthen family ties, as Marina described: *"[R]ecently, we have had family visits on my Nonna's side."* Lara commented: *"I have another cousin; actually, he was here fairly recently. He's been here once or twice in the last couple years."*

Conversely, no longer having family members living in Italy seemed to alter participants' experience of visits to Italy, as Marcelle lamented: *"But the sad thing is, now, I have no uncles and aunts, nothing, so I go back to Italy as a tourist. It's terrible."* When there are no familial connections, visits become mere holidays, without a sense of returning to one's own roots. It is having family members in Italy that makes Italy "home". Diego shared his positive experience: "*I feel, I feel actually at home. Very much.*" A similar sense was conveyed by Nadia: "*I feel completely at ease. I calm completely, because it is something I grew up with and it's familiar.*" Silvio described how visiting Italy for the first time he felt that he "*belonged*", adding "*and the people. They were like me. So this was the first time that I felt, okay, so I am not different, this is who I am.*"

However, there were instances when visits were experienced as challenging. Sandra noted that her first visit to Italy was not so easy:

> The country is a bit strange. It felt a bit, so ... [laughing] so, ja, it didn't feel like home; now when we came home [to South Africa], it was like, wow, this is home, and especially that time. When I went back then I actually had a different view but when I went at that time I felt very weird and out of place with the country. It didn't feel as beautiful and as lovely, [and] the people didn't feel as friendly as home.

Her Scottish, English-speaking husband was also overwhelmed on his first trip: "*It was very alien to him. He [...] doesn't understand the language, [...] he is very bad with languages, so no, shame ... [laughing] he didn't, he loved it, it was beautiful, but he was very much a foreigner there.*"

Beatrice commented on the challenges of not being familiar with the practicalities of Italian daily living: "*I felt like a stranger.... Yes, I remember she sent me out to buy – what was it – washing powder, and I could not think of the word in Italian for a top-loader.*" Other participants shared how their poor command of the Italian language contributed to a sense of alienation. Diego explained: "*They do recognize that, they say ..., so they can hear that I have a bit of an accent ... and also some of the terminology.*" A lack of fluency also added to a sense of not belonging for Carla: "*It was quite difficult for me because I didn't understand anything.*"

In the final analysis, regular visits to Italy in childhood play an important role in reinforcing second- and third-generation immigrants' sense of identity, as Nadia acknowledged: "*I think because I spent so much time in Italy and because the language and the culture [are] still so strong within me, I associate myself first with being Italian.*" In addition, we can see these visits as precursors to members of the second and third generations' "return" visits later in life. As we saw in Chapter 3, "return visits" are a journey that the descendants of the original immigrants undertake in order to find a sense of home and belonging in the country of their ancestors. In some instances, these return journeys may lead to a desire to move to Italy permanently.

Roots migration to Italy: fantasy or reality?

When we asked our participants whether they would consider moving to Italy on a more permanent basis, the question elicited a variety of responses and reflections.

Some second-generation immigrants considered moving to Italy; for example, Antonio, who wanted to complete his studies in Italy: *"So, I've always wanted to, you know, extend myself and go to Italy and study."* Those who spent more than just a brief holiday in Italy maintained a fairly idyllic view of their experience there. Marcelle described her experiences as follows: *"So that is what I loved. Wherever we went, there were [...] people that were passionate and happy and so much to talk about and read, and [they were] so knowledgeable."* Nino also gave a positive account:

> I lived in Italy for a couple of months and when I lived in Italy it was crazy because there they have those things on the piazza, where you go nights, ... We were just drinking wine, talking about ... oh what's the future holding for us ... and I just felt like I was in my element. So that's what I've noticed between living in South Africa and Italy.

Dario mentioned the difference in lifestyle between South Africa and Italy: *"I lived there for a month. ... I love the lifestyle. It's easy and all the family's there, even the ones that aren't; you know, you are kind of close."* It is significant that in these three examples, participants were describing fairly short-term experiences, although they spoke of "living in Italy".

There were, however, some pragmatic reflections on what living and working in Italy would entail in terms of the required language proficiency and navigating a professional network. Donatella, who had frequently travelled to Italy as a child, shared this view:

> Not to live. Do we love it on holiday? Absolutely. Would I maybe retire there one day? Yes, maybe that. Or go on big sabbaticals, but to live there. ... My first language is English. To work there is impossible. Anyway, not even the Italians are finding work. So ...

Professional challenges that could possibly be faced on moving to Italy were described by Matteo:

> But if you ask me now at age 55 to go and live in Italy, it's a system that I don't understand, that I can feel is different to what ..., to the life that I lead in South Africa, because in South Africa I have got a vast network.

There were some examples of second-generation participants who in the past had tried to move to Italy permanently for work purposes. It is of interest that in these instances they did not move in with family members who live in Italy, so this type of "roots migration" did not resemble the roots migration of the Australian second-generation immigrants described by Sala and Baldassar (2017), who reported that their participants moved to Italy with "the *explicit motivation* to return to and be with family (real and imagined)"

(p. 392, original emphasis). Our participants came to the realization that living in Italy was not the same as the idyllic holidays they had experienced as children. These sobering experiences eventually resulted in their return to South Africa. Charles shared his story, admitting that upon his return to South Africa, he had a renewed understanding of life and work in Italy:

> So that's why the period of living there was so valuable because it nuanced everything. Whereas before I had this sort of naïve nationalism. Living there, you know, woke me up to the deep, the deep imperfections in that society. [...] I can't imagine a nicer place to live on this planet, for me. And that's where I would definitely go and have a nice simple life in the country; go to Rome at the weekend, and that's what I would love to do, [...] but working there is impossible. It's difficult, let's not say it is impossible. ... It is a difficult life. My cousins have really struggled. They struggle to make ends meet and they work like dogs and they are always cleaning and ...

Tullio worked in Italy for a short time before returning to South Africa, commenting: "*I just felt that for me to open up a business there was very difficult and I found it was easier to open up a business in South Africa than over in Italy, yes.*"

The recognition that the experience of a holiday to Italy did not match the reality of day-to-day Italian life was encapsulated by Marcelle's words: "*I think Italy creates this fantasy about the ... beauty and the romance and whatever but the reality is something quite different.*"

Fabrizio, as a third-generation immigrant, considered spending some time there, but he was quite adamant that this would not be a permanent move, saying: "*I don't think I can live there.*" On the other hand, many of our third-generation participants openly expressed a desire to move to Italy permanently, even though most of them had a very limited Italian language proficiency. This aspiration was expressed by Angelo, who thought of the prospect of moving to Italy as a "*dream*" and elaborated: "*I'm considering it seriously [going to live in Italy], actually to be honest ... I want to get my Italian [...] sorted out.*" Marina agreed that she would need to improve her Italian before relocating: "*I ... definitely think about it, ... obviously [there is a] language barrier ... and I need to work on that.*" Both Lilla and Giulia were envisioning moving to Italy at some point. Silvio's motivation was closely linked to the fact that he still had family in Italy:

> Well, it is something I am thinking about a lot lately, just some prospects of going to go and, I have been always thinking about living and working [there]. I would love to, ... I think it is something I would love to do, ... could see some of the family is getting older and that's the last vestige that we actually have of any European connection, ... so I think that is

maybe why I feel like I want to go back there so that it still holds that connection true and that we don't lose that connection completely.

Some participants linked their desire to move to Italy to the socio-political difficulties South Africa is experiencing, as Carla mentioned: "*I, actually, ja, I think so because of the tension in this country.*" Ignazio also intimated that if the political and economic situation in South Africa worsens, moving to Italy would definitely become a consideration:

I still enjoy living there but when I … when it comes to that point where it's now not being enjoyable anymore or financially wise, it's not a good proposition anymore, then of course I will [go] over to … yes, I would definitely consider moving over to you to Italy.

These specific motivations can be seen as particular to the socio-political context of South Africa and reflect the general trend towards international out-migration that South Africa has witnessed since 1994 and which many have blamed on the political and economic situation in the country, including high levels of crime and corruption (Marchetti-Mercer, 2012; Marchetti-Mercer et al., 2020).

Susanna would have considered moving to Italy were it not that she was married with children and had a very strong attachment to her family of origin in South Africa. Therefore, she would not contemplate a move, not because of difficulties inherent to Italy but rather because of the larger implications for her family: "*See our problem as a family is – and maybe this is an Italian-ness – we are very close as a full family, [so] moving anywhere would involve moving everybody.*"

Laura's case was particularly significant, as her experience encapsulated a number of stories we have described thus far. She had a strong desire to live in Italy based on her childhood visits: "*I think growing up I obviously had this romantic idea, not only of living in Italy, but of marrying an Italian.*" However, when she eventually decided to go and live in Italy, she encountered a very different reality upon her arrival:

So what happened was, I moved. I moved to Italy, my dad came over with me to help me set up my life there. But because we didn't have family as a base, you know like you need a … you need a residential address to open … to get an ID book and open a bank account and you need … you need one thing to get this and you need this to get this to get that and we just couldn't get anywhere, so I couldn't even open a bank account. Because I didn't have a fixed address.

This had caused her to experience a strong sense of alienation, "*like I wasn't very rooted there. … You know and in Italy I couldn't, I couldn't quite figure out how things work."* As a result, Laura noted, *"I have never felt less Italian than I did in Italy."* This poignant reflection once again alerts us to the difference between an idealized view of Italy based on family holidays and, on the other hand, the harsh reality of day-to-day Italian life. It also points to the inevitable sense of estrangement that the younger generations may feel as they balance their sentiments of attachment to two countries, that of their forebears and the country of their own birth: *"I don't understand it, but it happens a lot, like I want to go now to Italy, but I know that through the weeks, I'll be like, no, I want to come back to South Africa. So I don't know, it's strange"* (Gabriella).

Conclusion

The childhood visits that we have described in this chapter can be defined as "family roots vacations" because they are undertaken by the immigrant family with the purpose of providing a cultural introduction to Italy and meeting remaining family members still living there, in the country of origin. These trips are thus deeply embedded in the concept of familyhood and emphasize the importance of emotional connections in transnational families. They also seem to have created an idealized view of Italy which served as a foundation for future visits and created a longing in some of our participants eventually to live in Italy permanently. In the final analysis this may create a particular type of nostalgia which we describe in more detail in the next chapter.

As we have seen, most participants were enthusiastic about their holidays in Italy because of the beauty of the country and the relaxed lifestyle they experienced. This enjoyment was strengthened by having family connections in Italy, making these trips particularly meaningful. In addition, picking up family connections reinforced their sense of Italian identity and belonging, as Nadia indicated: *"because I spent so much time in [Italy], I associate myself first with being Italian."* On the other hand, no longer having family members made Marcelle feel like a *"tourist"* when travelling to Italy.

The contradictions between an idealized as opposed to a realistic view of Italian society were evident in the different experiences of those of our participants who actually attempted to move to Italy on a more permanent basis. In these cases, our participants returned to South Africa with a deep sense of disillusionment. Laura's saddened comment that she *"never felt less Italian than [she] did in Italy"* was particularly striking. Thus, the idyllic memories of one's summer childhood holidays to Italy may be compared to a summer romance, as opposed to the realities of a long-term commitment.

References

Baldassar, L. (2001). *Visits home: Migration experiences between Italy and Australia.* Melbourne University Press.

Baldassar, L. (2011). Italian migrants in Australia and their relationship to Italy: Return visits, transnational caregiving and the second generation. *Journal of Mediterranean Studies, 20*(2), 255–282.

Baldassar, L. (2016a). Mobilities and communication technologies: Transforming care in family life. In M. Kilkey & E. Palenga-Möllenbeck (Eds.), *Family life in an age of migration and mobility* (pp. 19–42). Migration, Diasporas and Citizenship Series. Palgrave Macmillan.

Baldassar, L. (2016b). De-demonizing distance in mobile family lives: Co-presence, care circulation and polymedia as vibrant matter. *Global Networks, 16*(2), 145–163. https://doi.org/10.1111/glob.12109

Baldassar, L., Nedelcu, M., Merla, L., & Wilding, R. (2016). ICT-based co-presence in transnational families and communities: Challenging the premise of face-to-face proximity in sustaining relationships. *Global Networks, 16*(2), 133–144. https://doi.org/10.1111/glob.12108

Basu, P. (2004). Route metaphors of "roots tourism" in the Scottish Highland diaspora. In S. Coleman & J. Eade (Eds.), *Reframing pilgrimage: Cultures in motion* (pp. 150–174). Routledge.

Bryceson, D., & Vuorela, U. (2002). *The transnational family: New European frontiers and global networks.* Berg.

Horn, V. (2017). Migrant family visits and the life course: Interrelationships between age, capacity and desire. *Global Networks, 17*(4), 518–536. https://doi.org/10.1111/glob.12154

King, R., & Christou, A. (2010). Cultural geographies of counter-diasporic migration: Perspectives from the study of second-generation "returnees" to Greece. *Population, Space and Place, 16*(2), 103–119. https://doi.org/10.1002/psp.543

Levitt, P. (2002). The ties that change: Relations to the ancestral home over the life-cycle. In P. Levitt & M. C. Waters (Eds.), *The changing face of home: The transnational lives of the second generation* (pp. 123–144). Russell Sage Foundation.

Marchetti-Mercer, M. C. (2012). Is it just about the crime?: A psychological perspective on South African emigration. *South African Journal of Psychology, 42*(2), 243–254. ISSN 00812463. http://hdl.handle.net/2263/19278

Marchetti-Mercer, M. C., Swartz, L., & Baldassar, L. (2021). "Is Granny going back into the computer?" Visits and the familial politics of seeing and being seen in South African transnational families. *Journal of Intercultural Studies, 42*(4), 423–439. https://doi.org/full/10.1080/07256868.2021.1939280

Marchetti-Mercer, M. C., Swartz, L., Jithoo, V., Mabandla, N., Briguglio, A., & Wolfe, M. (2020). South African international migration and its impact on older family members. *Family Process, 59*(4), 1737–1754. https://doi.org/10.1111/famp.12493

Nesteruk, O., & Marks, L. (2009). Grandparents across the ocean: Eastern European immigrants' struggle to maintain intergenerational relationships. *Journal of Comparative Family Studies, 40*(1), 77–95. https://doi.org/10.3138/jcfs.40.1.77

Sala, E., & Baldassar, L. (2017). Leaving family to return to family: Roots migration among second-generation Italian-Australians. *Ethos, 45*(3), 386–408. https://doi.org/10.1111/etho.12173

Wessendorf, S. (2007). "Roots migrants": Transnationalism and "return" among second-generation Italians in Switzerland. *Journal of Ethnic and Migration Studies, 33*(7), 1083–1102. https://doi.org/10.1080/13691830701541614

8 "There is a lot of pain that I have inherited"

Identity through nostalgia

Introduction

When we are home, we do not need to talk about it, but when we are not at home, we may fall into a sense of nostalgia for home, a yearning, a pleasurable and yet sad longing. Boym (2001) captures this sense when she writes,

> "To be at home" – byt' doma – is a slightly ungrammatical expression in many languages. We just know how to say it in our native tongue. To feel at home is to know that things are in their places and so are you; it is a state of mind that doesn't depend on an actual location. The object of longing, then, is not really a place called home but this sense of intimacy with the world; it is not the past in general, but that imaginary moment when we had time and didn't know the temptation of nostalgia.
>
> (p. 251)

A more in-depth reflection on our findings suggests that there is a sense of nostalgia that is felt by our second- and third-generation participants towards Italy. At first glance, this sentiment may be surprising, since it is directed at a land of which they have had no direct experience other than holiday visits, and where the majority have not lived. Nostalgia is not always explicitly articulated as such, but it emerges as a *Leitmotif* nestled in the words and stories of our participants. Only one of them, Charles, described explicitly his relationship with Italy in terms that clearly express this sense:

> but there is a lot of pain. There is a lot of pain that I have inherited. There is a lot of melancholy and sadness about this, the separation. [...] Being away from home. And not... having a home in a sense, you know, in an identity sense. Just being different wherever you go.

Charles's comments on not "*having a home [...] in an identity sense*" reflects Boym's notion of a "sense of intimacy with the world". Home and identity are tied together. What is particularly significant in his reflection is the

DOI: 10.4324/9781003266884-8

acknowledgement of a *"pain"* that is *"inherited"* and which we explore in more detail in the course of this chapter.

Inherited nostalgia and identity

The word *nostalgia* has its roots in the Greek word *nostos*, which means return, and *algos*, which means pain: it is the pain associated with the desire of returning home. This return can be physical or metaphorical. Either way, nostalgia presupposes the existence of a "home" to which to return. However, when it comes to the second and third generations of immigrants, "home" is the original place from which the first generation came and not necessarily the "home" that their descendants have experienced, therefore making their nostalgia paradoxical, unless it is read in the light of Boym's (2001) comment, quoted above, about the recognition that nostalgia "is a state of mind that doesn't depend on an actual location" (p. 251).

In exploring the experiences of second-generation Iranian Americans, Maghbouleh (2010) found a type of "inherited nostalgia", which she defined as "the relational expressions of longing and belonging" (p. 214). She found that the nostalgia felt by the second-generation participants in her research was evident, for example, in their taste in music, which derived from their parents' accounts of their country of origin. This is also in line with Falicov's (2007) view that the relationships and attachments of migrants' descendants with the country of origin are not personal but are mediated by the memories and imaginations of one's forebears.

Our findings resonated with those of Maghbouleh (2010). Hence, we argue that Italian second- and third-generation immigrants in South Africa take on the nostalgia that is felt by the first generation and, therefore, they look towards Italy with similar feelings, not because of personal experiences, but because of what they have inherited from and through their parents and grandparents. In Chapter 5, we observed that we did not see any evidence of rebellion or rejection of the participants' parents' and grandparents' cultural values; instead, they seemed to greatly value the cultural identity markers to which they were exposed in their family of origin. Together with these values, they are also likely to have inherited a sense of nostalgia from first-generation immigrants.

This implies that second- and third-generation immigrants' nostalgia is not born out of a sense of "home" to which to "return", but rather, it is inherited from their parents and grandparents. It then creates an imaginary "home" to which they wish to "return". In other words, it is a reverse process, for it is not the existence of a distant "home" that evokes a sense of nostalgia but the existence of an inherited nostalgia that creates a distant "home", which is, however, imaginary. In addition, nostalgia makes it possible for second- and third-generation immigrants to live in this imaginary "home", as long as living in it is a symbolic act. This is performed by, for instance, maintaining traditions, transmitting memories, and taking an interest in various cultural identity markers, such as food preferences or sport team affiliation. On the other hand, when there is an actual physical "return", especially for periods longer than a month or two, this may sadly result in a deep sense of disillusionment, as we saw in Chapter 7.

Nostalgia from the past to the future

Nostalgia is based on memories from the past, but the sense of identity and belonging that it provides is rooted in the present. Rapone (2020) investigated the sense of *italianità* in descendants of people from Abruzzo who emigrated to three different countries, namely Australia, Canada, and the United States. She eloquently explains how nostalgia affects the present:

> Nostalgia and emotion are an embodied part of dealing with the past, and thus used when engaging about the past [...]. While it is understood that nostalgia can idealise the past, it can also imply optimism, where nostalgic memory can create a social cohesion among individuals who share a connection to a past, and by implication use their shared past to inspire them into the future [...].
>
> (Rapone, 2020, p. 64)

The feeling of sharing something from the past encourages migrants to think and conceptualize this past together, as a collective, rather than as an isolated individual. In this way, the nostalgia for and from the past becomes a meaningful feeling in the present: "Nostalgia helps them to construct the past by remembering and creating images to contrast with and provide meaning in the present" (Rapone, 2020, p. 94). Rapone (2020) found that what she describes as the "interconnectivity of emotion and nostalgia, through the maintenance of traditions" (p. 97) was a thematic thread in her data.

Similar conclusions may also be drawn from our participants' experiences, for whom the sense of nostalgia through which they talk about their experiences is not a passive longing for the past, which is impossible to recapture. Dario, for example, articulated this longing as a desire rooted in the present: "*But I ... every time there's something Italian here, I wish there was more.*" In this simple statement, Dario expresses a longing for something that should happen in the present – and possibly could also still happen in the future.

We should thus refrain from thinking that the nostalgic feeling is one exclusively connected to the past with possible consequences for the present. What we observed in our participants' stories is that their nostalgia was also characterized by a proactive and forward-looking attitude; in fact, nostalgia can help to create an imagination of the future. An example of this is the desire expressed by many of our younger third-generation participants to go and live in Italy, as described in Chapter 7. As we indicated, it was usually younger participants and those who had not lived in Italy for more than the span of a vacation who tended to have a romanticized idea of Italy as a place where they would like to go ("return") to live and work. Consequently, they tended to emphasize positive qualities associated with Italy, such as the food and lifestyle. They fantasized about the possibility of going to live in Italy based on these positive accounts and their holiday experiences. Despite such desires, significantly, only a few of them expressed the intention to live and work in Italy, because, for example, in Italy there might be more job opportunities for them, or because of other practical advantages such as better education or improved security, which are usually primary considerations for a migrant when moving to another country (Castelli, 2018). Job opportunities as a motivation to migrate have been shown to be particularly strong motivators for Italians, who, according to Cohen (2008), exemplify a labour diaspora.

Instead, what we see in our participants is evidence of an inherited nostalgia associated with their ancestors' country of origin, which presents itself with many positive, almost idyllic qualities, and therefore leads to a connected desire to live there in the near future. Nostalgia is what creates this desire and, consequently, it is a feeling projected towards the future. It creates an image based not only on one's own personal memories and experiences but even more strongly on the memories of one's parents and grandparents. It thus constructs an image of a place that does not really exist, as well as a desire to experience that place on a permanent basis.

Family memories from the past help to form a sense of identity and belonging in the present and are part of an imagined future. Nostalgia not only connects second- and third-generation Italian immigrants with a past through memories, and to the present through the construction of identity but also to the future through imagined possibilities. Second- and third-generation immigrants do not look at Italy as a place irremediably lost to them, as may be the case with the first-generation immigrants, but as a place to which it is possible to go "back".

Nostalgia and symbolic ethnicity

Through a number of cultural identity markers, participants are able to experience a metaphorical return. This is explicitly evident in how they described the importance that Italian food played in their family's life. Eating certain foods, cooked in a certain way, as was the tradition in the country of origin, potentially became a metaphorical going-back to the country of origin, recreating in the here and now the presence of the places left behind in immigrants' lives.

Teti, an Italian anthropologist who has devoted most of his research to migration, poignantly explains the emotional connotations that food holds for migrant populations:

Mangiare come nel luogo d'origine ha in qualche modo contribuito a placare la nostalgia, come se insieme al cibo e alle abitudini alimentari si fossero portati con sé nel nuovo mondo anche la casa, l'orto, i familiari, gli amici. Il cibo evoca e in qualche modo presentifica un luogo antropologico, fatto di parole, memorie, ricordi, storie, persone, relazioni.

(Teti, 1999, p. 90)

[Eating, like the place of origin, in some ways serves to placate nostalgia, eating habits together with food become nearly a way to bring with you into the new world your home, your vegetable garden, family members and friends. Food evokes and in some ways recreates an anthropological place made of words, memories, stories, people and relationships.]

(Own translation)

If food is a way of making present and materializing a distant anthropological place, through the foods of one's ancestors, the second and third generations can also then inhabit that place and, consequently, share the nostalgia for it. Once again, we see how immigrants are connected through nostalgia across generations and find a common "place" which they share. Nostalgia thus also provides a positive connotation and helps to negotiate one's own ethnic identity. It is not just an emotion, but a space of negotiation which becomes fundamental in order to build a sense of belonging. Since the majority of our participants' never actually resided in Italy, through this inherited nostalgia they have an opportunity to "live" there. In other words, by eating the same foods as their ancestors and feeling nostalgic about Italy, they emotionally recreate their ancestors' experience and, in doing so, build a sense of belonging to a place where they have never lived.

However, not every cultural marker is taken up, and not every cultural marker is linked to nostalgia; in other words, nostalgia does not come up indiscriminately with anything associated with Italy, and not everything associated with Italy, which gravitates around the construction of *italianità*, is used to build one's own sense of Italian identity. For example, as we saw in Chapter 6, the right to vote in the Italian national elections, and which may potentially contribute to a sense of political belonging, was not identified by our participants as an important part of their *italianità*.

This brings us to the debate around the concept of symbolic ethnicity (Gans, 1979) amongst the later generations of immigrants already outlined in Chapter 3. According to Gans (1979), who focused on the third generation, ethnic identity is voluntarily constructed by the descendants of immigrants when they select only some of the typical cultural markers associated with that specific ethnic identity, often the most pleasurable ones. The consequences of these selective choices result in third-generation immigrants creating a symbolic ethnicity rather than a "real" one. In other words, in order to create a symbolic affiliation to the ancestors' culture, what matters most is the adoption of individual ethnic markers such as food, rather than a complete or deeper acceptance of the ethnic identity. Gans (1979) regards nostalgia as a trigger factor in this process, which he describes as "a nostalgic allegiance to the culture of the immigrant generation, or that of the old country; a love for and a pride in a tradition that can be felt without having to be incorporated in everyday behavior" (p. 9). Gans's idea of symbolic ethnicity has been criticized by researchers such as Anagnostou (2009), Anderson (2016), and Sala (2017). They argue that Gans places too much emphasis on the voluntary aspect of taking on a specific ethnicity, without considering the constraints that can arise in accessing some of those cultural markers. He also seems to conceptualize ethnicity as a specific set of fixed (and thus essentializing) identity markers and makes an arbitrary distinction between superficial and "real" identity markers. His ideas suggest that it is only if one can display almost all, or at least the majority of, "real" cultural markers that one can be considered to be fully part of a particular ethnic group.

We do not see "symbolic" ethnicity as less "authentic" than a supposedly non-symbolic one; quite the contrary – the practices of the second- and third-generation immigrants in our research reveal that ethnicity potentially lies in a symbolic space altogether. This space is not a fixed one, as Gans (1979) seems to suggest, but is fluid and ever-evolving. Ethnicity is always symbolic, but there is a difference between Italians living in Italy and Italians in the diaspora. For those who live in Italy, there may be a more evident and clear parallel between their "symbolic" ethnicity and the place where they live. Consequently, their "symbolic" ethnicity adapts to the continuous evolution of Italian society. On the other hand, our South African–born participants construct their symbolic ethnicity in reference to an imagined place, based on inherited nostalgia.

The words of Teti (1999) can once again help us understand this process as follows:

> *L'emigrazione è stata considerata, a seconda dei diversi punti di vista, ora come elemento di "conservazione" ora come fenomeno di "rottura" dell'ordine tradizionale e gli emigrati sono stati descritti ora come inguaribili nostalgici ora come "ribelli" sempre irrequieti e insoddisfatti. In realtà nel movimento emigratorio continuità e mutamento, tradizione e innovazione, conservazione e trasformazione convivono, coesistono, s'incontrano e concorrono alla costruzione di un "ordine nuovo" rispetto a quello di origine, che comunque, reale o immaginario, vero o inventato, resta un ineludibile punto di riferimento e di "ritorno".*
> (pp. 576–577)

[Emigration has been considered, depending on different points of view, at times as a phenomenon of "preservation" and at times as a phenomenon of "rapture" and emigrants have been described as incurable nostalgics, and at times as "rebels" always restless and dissatisfied. In reality, in the migratory movement, continuity and change, tradition and innovation, conservation and transformation co-exist; they meet and work together towards the construction of a "new order" in respect of the original one, which in any case, whether real or imagined, real or invented, remains an unavoidable reference point and of "return".]

(Own translation)

Italian culture and aspects considered central to this culture, such as the importance of family, the beauty of the country, its historical and artistic heritage, food, and relaxed lifestyle, are viewed with a sort of bitter-sweet nostalgia by second- and third-generation Italians, and none of our participants, as already noted, expressed any overt criticism or opposition towards the cultural values they were exposed to in their families of origin. Nostalgia then also offers a way to build the imaginary homeland that these participants often associated with the geographical space of Italy but that does not really correspond with Italy as a political, cultural space today. It is, indeed, an imaginary place; however, it is not emotionally or psychologically less real than the physical place of Italy. It is towards this imaginary place that some of our participants would like to "return", because it is the place where they symbolically live and where they have constructed part of their identity. It is a place of belonging which is neither Italy nor South Africa.

Pillars of salt

A sense of nostalgia for their ancestors' land is not peculiar to second- and third-generation Italian immigrants living in South Africa; it is a common theme in Italian generations in other countries and in other nationalities across the globe as well. As already noted, food is generally one of the most common cultural markers associated with nostalgia, and with the attempt to recreate the "lost" country in both one's own family of origin and in the larger Italian community. Similarly, the myth of the "return" is also very widespread. It is certainly fed by the sense of nostalgia discussed above. However, as we noticed earlier, the nostalgia in our participants is one that does not only look at the past, and present, but also looks towards the future. Many of our participants acted on or were planning to act on this nostalgia by physically attempting to return to Italy, mainly mistaking Italy they will find once they get off the plane for the "Italy" on which they built part of their identity. Consequently, it is important to consider not only participants who contemplated going to live in Italy, but also the ones who tried to live in Italy and returned to South Africa with evident feelings of disillusionment. In other diasporic experiences, the return is either not physically possible (as in the case of refugees fleeing from war zones) or is not even contemplated (as may be the case of Italians living in the United States and Canada), but many of our Italian descendants deemed it to be a real option. This real possibility is also an important part of their ethnic identity and their sense of belonging.

Wessendorf (2007) observed something similar in second-generation Italians in Switzerland, although the participants in her research seemed to have more familiarity with Italy than our participants. In fact, they described regular, often annual, trips to their family's place of origin, which is obviously easier to achieve from Switzerland, given the geographical proximity, than when one lives in South Africa. Even so, Wessendorf (2007) noticed how second-generation Swiss Italians, once "back" in Italy, had to adapt and change the image and perception they held of Italy from an imagined one to a more realistic one. She conceptualizes this migration back to parents' homeland as a "root migration" which she defined as follows: "Italian roots migrants' connections to the homeland are based on everyday translocal ways of being and belonging during their childhood and adolescence" (Wessendorf, 2007, p. 1091). This definition does not apply to our South African participants in the same form – we cannot speak of a similar "roots migration". As already discussed, our participants' ethnic identity is constructed through certain cultural markers which do not generally require everyday practice; a salient example is that of language. Many deemed language very important in order to "be Italian", but many participants either did not speak it at all or were far from being fluent. It is for these reasons that we believe that the perceptions our participants have of Italy were much less based on elements of reality than on the imaginary.

Indian-born British-American author Salman Rushdie (1991), writing of his country of origin, India, articulated his sense of nostalgia acknowledging the risk associated with "looking back" and with the creation of "imaginary homelands":

> It may be that writers in my position, exiles or emigrants or expatriates, are haunted by some sense of loss, some urge to reclaim, to look back, even at the risk of being mutated into pillars of salt. But if we do look back, we must also do so in the knowledge – which gives rise to profound uncertainties – that our physical alienation from India almost inevitably means that we will not be capable of reclaiming precisely the thing that was lost; that we will, in short, create fictions, not actual cities or villages, but invisible ones, imaginary homelands, Indias of the mind.
>
> (p. 10)

Those among our participants who tried to live in Italy were indeed turned into "pillars of salt" as revealed in the stories of Charles and Laura. Acting on their nostalgia by going to Italy was a way of "looking back", not moving forward. It creates a paradox through which a nostalgic feeling is projected into the future while also taking one back into the past. However, as

Heraclitus already pointed out more than 2,000 years ago, it is not possible to step into the same river twice; it is impossible to travel back in time. There is a clash between the past and the future in the experiences of second- and third-generation South African Italian immigrants when they really attempt to go "back" to Italy. Feelings of estrangement and exclusion seemed to surface during these attempts.

Conclusion

We have analysed the feelings of nostalgia that emerge in the reflections of second- and third-generation Italians living in South Africa. Such nostalgia is not unique to our participants in the South African part of the Italian diasporas, but what is different for our participants is that this emotion often triggered a desire to go back to their ancestors' country, unlike, for example, for Italo-Americans, who see themselves as Americans first, and Italians second. This nostalgia extended across different timeframes: it is an emotion that comes from the past but pushes the second and third generations to look toward and act in the future. However, those who acted on it eventually realized (more or less consciously) that their attempt to move forward was in fact an impossible looking back: the destination turned out to be different from the imagined country that they had created for themselves.

Next, we explore in more detail how the desire to "return" was triggered not only by the attraction to Italy but also by the prevailing socio-political situation in South Africa. We describe a circular process where second- and third-generation Italians experienced a sense of nostalgia towards Italy because of an imaginary perception of Italy, and because they did not have a strong sense of belonging in present-day South Africa. Therefore, nostalgia is a cause which creates a new sense of belonging, but also a consequence of a feeling of non-belonging.

References

Anagnostou, Y. (2009). A critique of symbolic ethnicity: The ideology of choice? *Ethnicities, 9*(1), 94–122. https://doi.org/10.1177/1468796808099906

Anderson, C. V. (2016). Shame and pride in second-generation German identity in Melbourne, Australia: Emotions and white ethnicity. *Journal of Ethnic and Migration Studies, 42*(9), 1439–1454. https://doi.org/10.1080/1369183X.2015.1120660

Boym, S. (2001). *The future of nostalgia.* Basic Books.

Castelli, F. (2018). Drivers of migration: Why do people move? *Journal of Travel Medicine, 25*(1), tay040. https://doi.org/10.1093/jtm/tay040

Cohen, R. (2008). *Global diasporas: An introduction* (2nd ed.). Routledge.

Falicov, C. J. (2007). Working with transnational immigrants: Expanding meanings of family, community, and culture. *Family Process, 46*(2), 157–171. https://doi.org/10.1111/j.1545-5300.2007.00201.x

Gans, H. J. (1979). Symbolic ethnicity: The future of ethnic groups and cultures in America. *Ethnic and Racial Studies, 2*(1), 1–20. https://doi.org/10.1080/01419870.1979.9993248

Maghbouleh, N. (2010). "Inherited nostalgia" among second-generation Iranian Americans: A case study at a southern California university. *Journal of Intercultural Studies, 31*(2), 199–218. https://doi.org/10.1080/07256861003606382

Rapone, R. L. (2020). *Identity and intergenerational transmission of culture: A study of the Italian diaspora across three countries* [PhD dissertation, University of Sydney]. https://hdl.handle.net/2123/25381

Rushdie, S. (1991). *Imaginary homelands: Essays and criticism 1981–1991.* Granta.

Sala, E. (2017). *The Italian-ness is in the family: A critical evaluation of the role of family in constructions of ethnicity and connections to homeland among two cohorts of second generation Italian-Australians* [Doctoral dissertation, PhD thesis, University of Western Australia]. https://api.research-repository.uwa.edu.au/ws/portalfiles/portal/20507794/THESIS_DOCTOR_OF_PHILOSOPHY_SALA_Emanuela_2017.pdf

Teti, V. (1999). *Il colore del cibo: Geografia, mito e realtà dell'alimentazione mediterranea.* Meltemi.

Wessendorf, S. (2007). "Roots migrants": Transnationalism and "return" among second-generation Italians in Switzerland. *Journal of Ethnic and Migration Studies, 33*(7), 1083–1102. https://doi.org/10.1080/13691830701541614

9 "I don't feel Italian there and I don't feel South African here"

Finding belonging in an interliminal space

Introduction

We have seen that the sense of nostalgia felt by South African-born second- and third-generation Italians is instrumental in creating an imaginary place of belonging which they call "Italy", but which does not in fact correspond with the political and geographical realities of present-day Italy. If "belonging" is essentially a social construction, always referring to an imaginary place called "home" – this reminds us of the famous definition of a nation given by Anderson (1991), who sees it as an "imagined community" – in this chapter we argue that this is particularly the case for second- and third-generation Italians in South Africa.

Following on from our discussion on nostalgia, this chapter explores the desire – indeed, the need – for belonging expressed so poignantly by Probyn (1996):

> the desire that individuals have to belong, a tenacious and fragile desire that is [...] increasingly performed in the knowledge of the impossibility of ever really and truly belonging, along with the fear that the stability of belonging and the sanctity of belongings are forever past.
>
> (p. 8)

Belonging and *italianità*

Much has been written on the subject of belonging; we have chosen to focus on its socially constructed and ever-changing dimensions. We therefore view belonging as a form of attachment to a specific place, which is always constructed both by the self and by others. Belonging is continually becoming, developing. Like identity, it is never completely fixed in time and space. Yuval-Davis (2006) usefully identifies three levels of belonging:

> The first level concerns social locations; the second relates to individuals' identifications and emotional attachments to various collectivities and groupings; the third relates to ethical and political value systems

DOI: 10.4324/9781003266884-9

with which people judge their own and others' belonging/s. These different levels are interrelated, but cannot be reduced to each other, as so many political projects of belonging tend to assume.

(p. 199)

These three levels are interconnected and at the same time separate; they do not form a fixed unit. In our discussion in Chapter 6 on the political awareness and involvement of our participants, we saw that second- and third-generation Italians have little interest in voting in the Italian national elections and also attach little value to doing so. Most of the participants admitted that the Italian political system is too complicated to be understood from the outside; other constraints, such as limited language proficiency, made voting even more challenging. Sometimes participants even had difficulty remembering whether they had voted in the last election or not, and many disclosed that they had asked someone in the family for advice as to whom to vote for. Consequently, most of them did not see a link between voting rights and their belonging to Italy and their sense of *italianità*. Conversely, Yuval-Davis (2006) sees political belonging as important for identity, because it sets boundaries: "The boundaries that the politics of belonging is concerned with are the boundaries of the political community of belonging, the boundaries that separate the world population into 'us' and 'them'" (p. 204). One's right to participate in the political system of a country is a distinct way to influence what constitutes this set of boundaries.

In a study conducted on Italians living in London just before the law granting voting rights to Italians abroad was approved, Fortier (2000) found that these Italians were eager to have their own representation in Italy's parliament in order to be able to influence how Italy sees Italians abroad. In this instance, the question of identity and belonging was further complicated by a sense of belonging linked not only to Italy, but to Europe at large, which seems to be quite alien to the lived experiences of our South African participants. Given that 23 years have passed since Fortier's (2000) research, decades in which Europe and Europeanism have changed a lot, even for Italians living in Italy, it is interesting to note that among the second- and third-generation immigrants in South Africa that we interviewed, Italy is not spoken about in the context of a broader European identity. The fact that the original immigrants left Italy prior to the rise of the European Union may contribute to the narrower construction of Italy among their descendants.

It is evident that, as far as our participants are concerned, their sense of Italian identity or *italianità* did not include a focus on political belonging. It was not their ability to vote in an Italian national election that defined their sense of identity. Even Italian citizenship, which all of them held, did not seem to add value to their sense of *italianità*. Instead, they appreciated their dual citizenship for the pragmatic advantages that this position offers, for example, in terms of the ease of international travel. However, as we have already discussed, it was evident that they attached considerable importance to the Italian language when it came to their sense of *italianità*: although most of them were not able to speak it fluently (or at all), they did not feel less "Italian" if they could not speak it. This reveals an ambivalent relationship towards the Italian language as a cultural marker. On the one hand, there was a tremendous appreciation for the language, as well as a desire to learn the language or improve proficiency; on the other hand, whether they could speak Italian or not did not seem to have much influence on their sense of *italianità*.

These examples reveal two important aspects of our participants' sense of belonging. The first is that belonging is not necessarily linked to elements that one possesses or does not possess, but rather to more imaginary concepts. The evidence in our research suggests that the construction of belonging is linked to an ideal, rather than to objective and material factors, even if the relevance of such factors should not be ignored. In other words, objective and material aspects certainly matter, but they are not fundamental to creating a sense of belonging or *italianità*. Our participants did not feel Italian because of the Italian passport they held or the right to vote in the Italian national elections, but they did feel Italian because of the acknowledged role of the Italian language in their lives, although most of them did not speak it or they had a very limited competence. Their Italian belonging was therefore built on considerations that can be quite contradictory. However, as we explained in the previous chapter regarding symbolic ethnicity, one should refrain from judging or labelling this sense of belonging as less authentic or real because of these contradictions; rather, we should recognize that it is a construction. Hence, belonging is never automatic or "objective".

The second point we wish to emphasize is that the sense of belonging of second- and third-generation Italian immigrants is not built on the current realities of today's Italy, but rather on an imagined Italy, as we already saw in the previous chapter, which can also further explain why political belonging is not really relevant to them. Political belonging means participation in the public affairs of a specific country, which is strongly linked to the political and social realities of that country. Although political belonging, like all types of belonging, is an abstraction, it is inextricably entwined with elements that are real, such as voting in elections, political debate and legislation. Our research participants do not construct their sense of belonging based on elements verifiable in reality; for this reason, language can be considered an important element for identity, even if it is not spoken: what matters most is not speaking Italian, but gravitating towards it and acknowledging its role in one's life.

This specific construction of belonging and identity needs to be understood in the unique context of South Africa.

The "Italian game" in South Africa

Some participants described a feeling of being "different" from other South Africans, because of their Italian origins. For example, Silvio related:

> I do recognize, I am different, I am starting … I think later on, I started to accept that I am South African and that's an identity, but for a long part, it has been very much about where am […] there, there is a strong heritage in terms of … because growing up, you knew, you were labelled as Italian. So you had that label and you still have that connection that that is part of your identity.

Gabriella spoke extensively about the difference of being Italian in South Africa:

> My best friend's Italian, my boyfriend's Italian. I mean there's just something different in the way that we see things. Our mentality is quite diverse as opposed to [that of] my South African friends […] Yes, all the time. I just, I can't integrate into a group of people because my ways are very different to their ways. So they look at me weird and they say to me, why aren't you doing what we're doing, and I just don't wanna do it […] obviously just the sense of belonging that I feel when I'm there, and I just feel like I'm part of it, whereas here, I feel a little bit outside of the culture. I don't know, I don't seem to integrate myself well.

The idea of not belonging and of being different in South Africa seems to be a more prominent theme in the third generation. One of them, Carla, connected the idea of being different with the idea of not being like other white South Africans:

> Ja, so ja, but I feel like I am a mixture of everything. I'm not just one identity, ja, and I enjoy that, because I think in South Africa especially, everyone says that, you know. There's a whole politic[al] thing involved, but you know, everyone's got a mixture of everything in them and to me I might just look like a white person, but I'm actually not really South African. I was born here, but I'm not really South African. My roots are all over the place, so ja, so I really enjoy that about myself. And I still call myself proudly South African because I was born here, but I have a whole lot of roots.

Carla's experience is common to many of the participants. In different ways, many of our participants spoke of being Italian as differentiating them from white South Africans in South Africa. However, this did not translate into a complete sense of belonging when they were in Italy. Donatella, for example, said: *"I wish I was more Italian when I am in Italy."* Laura echoed a similar situation: *"And then you go to Italy and you are not Italian because you weren't born there."* Beatrice recounted feeling like a stranger when visiting Italy and being sent out to buy washing powder, and being unable to remember the Italian word for a top-loader washing machine: *"It just couldn't come to me and I couldn't, and when I got home my granny didn't seem to understand either – what was I going on about? And ... [laughing] so, yes I felt like a stranger."* She elaborated on her ambivalent feelings with regard to belonging in Italy: *"Sort of belong, yes. Yes, I belong kind of, how can we say ..., we belong because we are wearing the same uniform, but we don't belong because we are not playing the game."*

These comments on "playing the game" may be related to Bourdieu's (1986) observation on capital: "It is what makes the games of society – not least, the economic game – something other than simple games of chance offering at every moment the possibility of a miracle" (p. 241). He uses the term capital not only as an economic concept but also as a social and cultural one. Cultural capital in particular is made up of an embodied state, "in the form of long-lasting dispositions of the mind and body" (Bourdieu, 1986, p. 243), an objectified state, "in the form of cultural goods" (Bourdieu, 1986, p. 243), as well as an institutionalized state, which encompassed the institutional and public recognition of cultural capital, for example, in the form of a university degree. The embodied type of cultural capital is acquired over time – it cannot be immediately transmitted like money – both through an action of self-improvement and through family transmission. In our study, we can see an Italian heritage as part of this embodied cultural capital. If we understand Beatrice's comment in relation to Bourdieu, we can see how Beatrice might come to feel as though she is not playing *"the game"* because her cultural capital does not equip her sufficiently to play the "games of Italian society". She might wear the *"same uniform"* (an Italian name, passport, parents), which gives the impression of belonging to that specific team, but in fact she does not know the rules fully enough to play the game well. Therefore, in the case of second- and third-generation Italian immigrants in South Africa, the cultural capital linked to the Italian heritage does not provide them with sufficient knowledge of the rules and norms of Italian society; at the same time this capital disenables them from participating fully in the "games" played in South Africa.

Marino (2019), in his research on the sense of identity in three generations of Italian migrants in Australia, connects Bourdieu's theory to the concept of a double absence, a dualism that arises amongst migrants where "individuals can be simultaneously considered 'foreigners' (or strangers) in their country of origin because they no longer live there, as well as in the dominant society, too, where metaphorically they do not really 'have a place'" (pp. 709–710). Marino (2019) observes that both the first and the second generations of Italians in Australia experienced this sense of double absence, as is shown by the fact that they did not feel either Australian or Italian. However, the third generation experienced their Italian origin in a more positive way and considered "being Italian as cool", as we discussed in Chapter 3. According to Marino (2019), this shift may be partially attributed to a change in the attitude of the dominant Australian society towards Italian immigrants, who were previously not considered "white enough", but who have now have been completely assimilated into the dominant society's definition of being "white". (The "whiteness" motif may apply to some degree to our participants, but may not apply to other second- and third-generation people of Italian descent in South Africa, particularly those of mixed descent.)

Marino's (2019) findings speak to ours in a very meaningful way. On the one hand, all our participants perceived being Italian as a positive feature of their identity, which was exemplified, as we saw in Chapter 5, in strong pride regarding their Italian origins. However, this sense of pride did not translate into feeling more at home in South Africa, as in the case of the third-generation Italian-Australians interviewed by Marino.

As we noted in Chapter 3, a migrant's sense of belonging in the destination country depends strongly on "how receptive the host culture is and what its political and social policies regarding cultural integration are" (Sala, 2017, p. 34). South Africa is a country characterized – and racked – by cultural and ethnic differences. After the first democratic elections in 1994, the prevailing rhetoric envisaged national unity through the metaphor of the rainbow nation. Unlike the American "melting pot" construct, where the idea is that different origins are combined to become a unified identity, in the South African project differences were celebrated, allowing groups to remain distinct but equally important. There was therefore no national assimilation project; instead, prominence was given to the idea of difference. The concept of a "rainbow nation" has since come under fire for not addressing sufficiently issues of structural racism and inequalities still present in South African society. Consequently, South Africa has not developed a strong notion of national identity and, coming from a long era of oppression, first in the form of colonialism and then in the form of apartheid, the idea of a South African identity is still the site of much political and social contention:

> Today, the concept of the Rainbow Nation, the central metaphor for post-apartheid South Africa, falls short of serving as a broadly acknowledged identity marker. In essence, the concept's validity expired due to its implied impetus to downplay the existence of contrasting living realities from diversified identities, thus glossing over sustained systemic discrimination and inequality.
>
> (Turner, 2019, p. 81)

One may therefore argue that South Africa today is a nation that is still looking for an identity. In consequence, whereas Italians in Italy, for example, may have a reasonably similar, shared idea of what it means to be Italian (although nationalist concepts per se are not without theoretical difficulty), many South Africans do not find it easy to explain what it means to be South African. The picture becomes even more complicated when, instead of referring to South Africans in general, we talk about specific ethnic and racial groups. For instance, the concept of "whiteness" has undergone a notable change from the apartheid era to today. Even though white people still benefit from many accumulated privileges from the past, the main national discourse about being white has changed considerably. Today being white in South Africa comes not only with inherited economic and social privileges but also with a sense of guilt about the past (Vice, 2010).

As we saw in Marino's Australian research, which is not an isolated case, the categorization of Italians as white has been the source of an extensive – and often subtle – debate. Even though Italy, since its inception as a nation in 1861, has always tried to construct its own identity as white (Virga, 2019), Italians have not always been seen as white in other national contexts (for a more in-depth exploration of Italian's history in the United States, as a case in point, see Allen, 1994; Roediger, 2005). In South Africa, during the apartheid era, most Italians enjoyed all the economic and social privileges of being white, although being predominantly Catholic rather than Protestant made them dissimilar from the majority of white people in the country, together with other European migrants, such as Portuguese immigrants.

The end of the apartheid regime "created something of an identity crisis for many white South Africans. Being white seemed to carry with it significant taint and some white South Africans responded to this by declaring themselves to be African" (Matthews, 2015, p. 113). Since 1994, white people in present-day South Africa are still grappling with their sense of identity and trying to redefine themselves and find a place, a way to fit in, in the current society (Steyn, 2001). We then need to understand the sense of identity and belonging of Italian second and third generations in this racialized and re-racialized context.

While Italians, as white people in general, in South Africa are trying to look for a new identity, compared to other South African white people, they can leverage their Italian cultural heritage as one that does not come from Africa as a mark of difference, and as belonging at the same time. It could be for that reason that all our participants, although in different ways and to different degrees, felt a sense of belonging in Italy. For them, Italy is not only the homeland of their ancestors but also a homeland where they can live and ideally feel "at home" in a context in which in their own country of birth – South Africa –has become potentially challenging. This is in contrast to other white people of European descent, most notably the Afrikaners (descendants of the original Dutch colonialists but usually multiple generations later) who often argue that they do not have any European country to go back to, which makes them uniquely African (Steyn, 2004).

At the same time, as we saw earlier, belonging to Italy comes with challenges of its own, especially in relation to present-day Italy. The second- and third-generation Italian immigrants' reflections on Italian popular culture and Italian affairs revealed a lack of prominent Italian role models in South Africa, as well as the absence of an established and well-developed Italian-South African culture. The second and third generations of Italians in South Africa, therefore, cannot look inwards towards the country of their own birth in order to find a niche in which to build their own particular identity. Consequently, they seem to look directly towards Italy, taking their cultural point of reference from there and constructing in their imagined Italy the sense of their partial belonging, through nostalgia, as discussed in Chapter 8. However, as we have already pointed out, the image of the "homeland" constructed in this way remains an imaginary one, which crumbles upon contact with real-life experiences. Therefore, there is no public-level construction of an Italian-South African identity.

Interliminality

We argue that the constructed identity of second- and third-generation Italians in South Africa is not based on a double *absence* but is instead built on an imagined *presence* in what we want to describe as an interliminal space.

The idea of liminality comes from anthropology. Victor Turner (1969) describes the state of liminal being as

> necessarily ambiguous, since this condition and these people elude or slip through the network of classifications that normally locate states and positions in cultural space. Liminal entities are neither here nor there; they are betwixt and between the positions assigned and arrayed by law, custom, convention and ceremonial.
>
> (p. 95)

By contrast, interliminality is a concept used in translation studies. It was originally coined by Rose (1997) to describe the space between a text and the subsequent texts that derive from it, whether in the form of translations or adaptations. She contends that "a translation challenges our reading by giving it a boundary. But in setting this provisional boundary, a translation also establishes an interliminal space of sound, allusion, and meaning where we must collaborate, criticize, and rewrite" (Rose, 1997, p. 86). The interliminal space is thus potentially a very productive space where new meaning can be created, meaning that does not derive from only one text but has both (or more) texts as references. As Culler (2010) notes, it is an "interliminal space of possible meanings: attempting a translation helps us discover what the source text might mean – which is faithful to the most elementary use of translations to discover the meaning of texts we cannot read in the original"

(p. 95). Duff (1981) uses the term "third language" to speak about translating from one language into another: according to him, the translator does not move between two languages, but in fact creates a third one. This notion is taken up by Robert-Foley (2016), who defines this third language as an interliminal space, the potentiality of which she highlights in terms of productivity.

A liminal space, as described in anthropology, gives the sense of a transitional space between one status and another. Bhabha (1994), in postcolonial theory, refers to an in-between space of exchange, meeting, and potential subversion. Interliminality, on the other hand, conveys the idea of a space constructed not as a transitory space, or space of transition, but as a space that is inhabited permanently, albeit in the realm of a symbolic world. This is not to say that it is a fixed and unchangeable space, but that it has the characteristics of something made to be stable, to be used as a metaphor. Rather than the threshold of a door (a liminal space) between two rooms, it is a room between two thresholds. The analogy of translation seems particularly apt in attempting to understand the experiences of second- and third-generation migrants, as migrations can also be seen as translating one's life experiences from one world to another.

We argue that the Italian second and third generations in South Africa find their sense of belonging in such an interliminal space, constructed between Italy and South Africa: in terms of the construction of their identity, they are not really South African, but not yet (or no longer) Italian, or not really Italian, but not yet South African. The difference between this concept and the idea of transnationalism is that this identity is not built by taking cultural markers from both countries but rather by creating a third imaginary space, as we saw in the previous chapter. This is not a hybrid or contrapuntal identity, as discussed in Chapter 3, because of its many imagined elements. Although we do not deny that our participants have transnational experiences, we also recognize that their constructed identity does not refer to both national identities. As a consequence, many participants admitted to a feeling of estrangement when in Italy, and at the same time a feeling of not completely belonging to South Africa. Although at first glance this construction of identity may seem based on a fantasy, and therefore not real, we must remember that every construction of identity is always symbolic. Furthermore, we must refrain from viewing it in a negative light as in the case of the "symbolic identity" critiqued by Gans (1979). Returning to the origin of the concept of interliminality in translation studies, we should instead emphasize the potential creativity and meaning that this construction of identity may hold.

Conclusion

The idea of a third space as a different space created by migrants has been recently proposed, building on Bhabha's and Soja's works (Purkarthofer, 2022), as a way to move away from the binarity between the country of origin and the destination country. However, the construction of a third space is still seen, in relation to these two countries, as something in between the two. Introducing the idea of an interliminal space may help us to conceptualize a space that is not between the two reference points but somewhere else in the psychological and symbolic world. In this space, the often-contradictory actions and beliefs that we observed in many of our participants, such as the importance ascribed to the Italian language despite a lack of linguistic competence, or holding an Italian passport without political participation, may be reconciled. Furthermore, the concept of interliminality helps us to see this space as a more permanent one: it is not a place of passage, therefore liminal, but a place in which to live and build one's own "safe" sense of belonging. Therefore, we maintain that although a culture definable as Italian-South African is not evident, second- and third-generation Italian immigrants in South Africa have rather created a space called "Italy" from which to perform their own cultural and identity markers.

References

Allen, T. (1994). *The invention of the white race*. Verso.

Anderson, B. (1991). *Imagined communities: Reflections on the origin and spread of nationalism*. Verso.

Bhabha, H. K. (1994). *The location of culture*. Routledge.

Bourdieu, P. (1986). The forms of capital. In J. G. Richardson (Ed.), *Handbook of theory and research for the sociology of education* (pp. 241–258). Greenwood Press.

Culler, J. (2010). Teaching Baudelaire, teaching translation. *Profession*, 91–98. Retrieved from http://www.jstor.org/stable/41419865

Duff, A. (1981). *The third language: Recurrent problems of translation into English: It ain't what you do, it's the way you do it*. Pergamon.

Fortier, A.-M. (2000). *Migrant belongings. Memory, space, identity*. Routledge.

Gans, H. J. (1979). Symbolic ethnicity: The future of ethnic groups and cultures in America. *Ethnic and Racial Studies*, *2*(1), 1–20. https://doi.org/10.1080/01419870.1979.9993248

Marino, S. (2019). Ethnic identity and race: The "double absence" and its legacy across generations among Australians of Southern Italian origin. Operationalizing institutional positionality. *Ethnic and Racial Studies*, *42*(5), 707–725. https://doi.org/10.1080/01419870.2018.1451649

Matthews, S. (2015). Shifting white identities in South Africa: White Africanness and the struggle for racial justice. *Phronimon*, *16*(2), 112–129. https://doi.org/10.25159/2413-3086/3821

Probyn, E. (1996). *Outside belongings*. Routledge.

Purkarthofer, J. (2022). Transnational families' social spaces "in between": Expectations, decision-making and belonging in light of educational choices in Norway. *European Educational Research Journal*, *0*(0). https://doi.org/10.1177/14749041221106846

Robert-Foley, L. (2016). Writing with translational constraints: On the "spacy emptiness" between languages. *MLN*, *131*(4), 905–918. https://doi.org/10.1353/mln.2016.0065

Roediger, D. R. (2005). *Working towards whiteness: How America's immigrants became white.* Basic Books.

Rose, M. G. (1997). A sentimental education: Exploring the interliminal translation theory and postmodern taste. *Dalhousie French Studies, 38* (Meaning and manner: From Marie de France to Marie-Claire Blais, Mélanges de littérature présentés à Rostislav Kocourek par ses collègues et élèves, Spring), 85–93. https://www.jstor.org/stable/40837151

Sala, E. (2017). *The Italian-ness is in the family: A critical evaluation of the role of family in constructions of ethnicity and connections to homeland among two cohorts of second generation Italian-Australians* [Doctoral dissertation, PhD Thesis, University of Western Australia]. https://api.research-repository.uwa.edu.au/ws/portalfiles/portal/20507794/THESIS_DOCTOR_OF_PHILOSOPHY_SALA_Emanuela_2017.pdf

Steyn, M. (2001). *Whiteness just isn't what it used to be.* SUNY Press.

Steyn, M. E. (2004). Rehabilitating a whiteness disgraced: Afrikaner *white talk* in post-apartheid South Africa. *Communication Quarterly, 52*(2), 143–169. https://doi.org/10.1080/01463370409370187

Turner, I. (2019). Axing the rainbow. *Modern Africa: Politics, History and Society, 7*(1), 81–110. https://doi.org/10.26806/modafr.v7i1.244

Turner, V. (1969). *The ritual process: Structure and anti-structure.* Cornell University Press.

Vice, S. (2010). How do I live in this strange place? *Journal of Social Philosophy, 41*(3), 323–342. https://doi.org/10.1111/j.1467-9833.2010.01496.x

Virga, A. (2019). African "ghosts" and the myth of "Italianness": The presence of migrant writers in Italian literature. *Tydskrif vir Letterkunde, 56*(1), 102–112. https://doi.org/10.17159/2309-9070/tvl.v.56i1.6276

Yuval-Davis, N. (2006). Belonging and the politics of belonging. *Patterns of Prejudice, 40*(3), 197–214. https://doi.org/10.1080/00313220600769331

10 Conclusion

Coming to the end of the writing of this book feels like the end of the journey. Although at the beginning of the project, we had a specific destination in mind, we found ourselves taking a number of different routes, which took us into unexpected territory. Such productive detours are common in an academic project, and they definitely applied in this study. As we mentioned at the start of the book, we set out with the intention of exploring the sense of *italianità* in second-generation Italian immigrants living in South Africa. The original idea was to address a gap in scholarly research in this area, compared to other, much more fully explored, Italian diasporas in the world. However, as we embarked on the project, a number of younger third-generation immigrants contacted us. One might argue that despite the fact that their connection with Italy was very diluted, they were very enthusiastic about our project and were keen to share their stories with us, which led us to broaden the scope of our investigation.

At the same time, our data collection process was made difficult by a number of challenges, including financial and logistical limitations, exacerbated by the COVID-19 pandemic, which severely restricted both our personal and professional lives.

As part of our research, we accessed many international works on the experiences of Italian migrants and their descendants in other countries, especially the United States and Australia. These diasporas have been researched in depth. A number of scholars in the social sciences and humanities have also explored various acculturation strategies available to these groups. We also looked at recent trends in transnationalism and youth mobility today. While this vast body of academic work was very useful to help us plan our research and to give us a theoretical orientation, as we began writing this book, we soon realized that we were looking at a different type of migration.

Pride in being Italian, the importance of Italian family values, and a romanticized image of Italy itself are just a few of the most prominent features of the second and third generations of Italians in South Africa. They have these traits in common with other Italian diasporas internationally. However, a deeper analysis of the meaning behind these characteristics revealed that the motivations and consequences of what we could define as a superficial and common

DOI: 10.4324/9781003266884-10

aspect of *italianità* are profoundly different from those in other contexts. We have therefore traced differences and peculiarities unique to the South African historical, political, and social context which cannot be compared to the situation in other Anglophone countries.

Furthermore, our study looks at migration from the Global North to the Global South, and in some instances, from other parts of Africa to South Africa. This is a very different trend than that usually discussed in the literature. As the historical overview of the Italian presence in South Africa shows, World War II was a strong catalyst for Italian immigration to South Africa. Many of today's second- and third-generation Italians in South Africa are descended from Italian prisoners of war in South Africa who either decided to remain in South Africa or, after briefly returning to Italy following the end of the war, came back to South Africa shortly thereafter, many bringing their families along. This is a unique migratory path. Although these Italians moved for a very common reason – the hope of jobs and better life conditions – they did not leave Italy without knowing what to expect in the destination country, and they consciously chose South Africa as a destination because they had already experienced and liked it. In the decades following the end of the war, many other Italian immigrants came to South Africa from other African countries, creating other unique migratory paths, partially linked to the end of the Italian colonial enterprise in Africa. Although these Italians still retained the Italian language and a strong connection with Italy, they felt more comfortable about immigrating to another African country than about going to Italy.

In exploring the larger body of literature on second- and third-generation immigrants, we encountered a number of theories that attempt to shed light on the relationships that such groups have with their forebears' countries of origin, as well as with the countries where they were born. In the last few decades, increasing ease of mobility and the rapid evolution of information and communication technologies have changed the relationship between migrant families and the country left behind. In the beginning, we considered transnationalism and mobility to be useful lenses to understand our participants' sense of *italianità*. However, once we began analysing our data, we realized that these concepts did not seem to capture an important aspect of our participants' identity, namely their struggle with a sense of belonging, as well as their strong nostalgia towards what appears to be a fairly imaginary notion of Italy. Their sense of being unsettled led us to examine in more depth what our participants' relationship with Italy and South Africa entailed.

In the apartheid years, South Africa practised a strongly politicized, artificial categorization of different population groups. Most Italians fell into the category of whites and enjoyed a number of the same privileges as other white South Africans, but there was no single South African society to assimilate into, as in the case of the purported "melting pot" in the United States. There were strong cultural differences between Italian immigrants and white English-speaking South Africans, and even more with the descendants of the original Dutch colonialists, the Afrikaners, with their strong Calvinistic roots. Some Italians married people from local indigenous groups and some of their descendants were not classified as white. Furthermore, even if Italians were white, they were still not seen as white in the same way as those of English or Afrikaner descent; they could therefore enjoy the privileges of being white but did not easily fit into the dominant white society.

With the end of apartheid and the beginning of a new democracy, a new way of being "South African" arose in the form of the "rainbow nation", as discussed in Chapter 9. This construct of national identity was based on a call to respect and value differences, and on the dream that distinct groups of people can live in harmony without giving up their individual and cultural differences. However, nearly 30 years have passed since the advent of democracy and criticism around the viability of the rainbow nation is severe. The construct is lambasted because it does not address the structural differences in South African society that have led to deep inequalities, which have intensified, rather than being resolved. Descendants of the original Italian immigrants have to negotiate their identity in this highly charged, complex political and social context.

We argue that the second- and third-generation Italian immigrants ascribed significance to their Italian roots as a response to the challenges of belonging posed by South African society. Although only a few of our respondents were truly fluent in Italian, they greatly valued the role of the Italian language in their sense of *italianità* and often expressed a desire to learn the language or improve their proficiency. They fondly recalled family meals, as well as the celebration of traditional holidays, and they displayed a strong sense of pride in their Italian origins. They saw no sense in rebelling against the values and traditions of their Italian forebears. In fact, they seemed to value how these values and traditions had contributed to the richness of their lives. Visits to Italy were initiated during childhood as a form of cultural introduction, and such visits evoked very strong and fond memories. Consequently, at some point, many participants considered moving to Italy permanently; to us as researchers, this option seemed less likely, given the lack of Italian proficiency of many of these participants. Their nostalgia and connection to Italy was mostly linked to their family roots vacations rather than other more material identity markers, such as citizenship. Having an Italian passport and being able to vote in the national elections were rarely mentioned, if at all, as something that made them feel particularly Italian: in fact, these markers of citizenship seemed to be mainly a practical benefit, allowing for ease of travelling. Their understanding of Italian politics and Italian current affairs seemed in most cases to be superficial and something they did not explore adequately, despite access to the international Italian television station, newspapers, and online news.

One of the most interesting aspects of this construction of *italianità* is that it was strictly linked to a sense of belonging. As we have argued, some of these traits may seem common to the descendants of Italian immigrants in other countries, but in South Africa they are functional primarily in creating a sense of belonging. In other words, *italianità* is not only an origin that determines selected specific characteristics (for example, as a superficial marker, traditional family Sunday lunches) but also an identity that gives access to a specific sense of belonging while living in a country where belonging is a challenging and sometimes even a contested aspect of life. This contestation relates to the fact that "whiteness" in South Africa has become an uncomfortable identity, negatively associated with the country's history of apartheid. There seems to be a need and a desire among younger white immigrants' descendants to differentiate themselves from the political choices that were made in the country in the past. Consequently, emphasizing Italian roots may be helpful in this process. In addition, as Marino (2021) has also found, being Italian abroad seems to have become "cool", as the strong "Made in Italy" brand has gained more traction internationally.

For our participants, *italianità* is nurtured by nostalgia. As we have shown in Chapter 8, this is often an inherited nostalgia acquired from their parents and grandparents. Nostalgia also serves as a way to create an imaginary version of Italy where they can feel they belong. We propose that the sense of belonging which derives from this constructed *italianità* can be understood through the conceptual lens of interliminality. This construct derives from the field of translation studies, and we were deeply drawn to it, based on our own personal experiences as migrants. We often found ourselves translating our own lived experiences – indeed, often our lives – from one culture to another.

Our participants' sense of identity did not seem to be appropriately captured by what Sala (2017) refers to as a hybrid or contrapuntal model, but rather as an interliminal one, which is based on belonging in an imaginary third space. Interliminality speaks to and about a symbolic place which is neither in-between nor transitory but is stably constructed in the intersection of two spaces (in this case, South Africa and Italy). However, this space is unique; it is different from both of these countries. Unlike, for example, the Italo-American culture, which has its origins in Italy but is rooted in the United States, the interliminal space constructed in South Africa and called "Italy" does not have roots in South Africa, where indeed, as we noticed, there is no Italian-South African culture with its own specificities. For example, there are no appropriate role models, typical cuisine, unique celebrations or traditions (such as the now-controversial Columbus Day in the United States).

At the end of our research journey, we would argue that the *italianità* constructed in South Africa differs from the *italianità* constructed elsewhere, in other Italian diasporas or in Italy itself. Descendants of Italian immigrants to South Africa define themselves using only selected cultural markers, such as food, art, and ancient history. Other features associated with life in Italy are completely ignored; for example, an impenetrable bureaucracy, characterized by its own specific difficult language, a contested past made up of internal colonialism and colonialism towards other territories, memories of the civil war between fascist and anti-fascist supporters that developed after 1943, to name but a few. Our participants did not take up this part of the more recent Italian heritage into their sense of *italianità*. Nor do they deem current Italian political debates relevant – they dismiss the Italian political system as too complicated to be understood from the "outside".

Every diasporic context is different and evokes a different response in terms of identity and belonging. Therefore, we would argue that, in the same way, every diaspora may develop its own idea of Italy. The ancestors' homeland is always an imagined one, whether or not it allows, as in our case, for the development of a sense of belonging – what is different in each diaspora is how this imaginary place is constructed. There are as many "Italies" as there are diasporas (Gabaccia, 2000). Each of these Italies probably mirrors the diaspora from which this imaginary space arises. More research is needed in this area; it would be helpful to investigate how the construction of the imaginary homeland depends on the diasporic context, and also how it may influence the adaptation of immigrants to their destination countries.

Further research should also investigate the first-generation Italian migrants to South Africa, who were omitted from this study. Since we have discovered that the second and third generations inherited their nostalgia from their family of origin, it would be appropriate to analyse how the first generation created and transferred this nostalgia in the first place. Such research should be undertaken sooner rather than later, as the first generation is ageing rapidly, and many have already passed away.

Something that also emerged from the research, but that was not a focus at the inception of the study, is the question of how race as a component of the immigrant experience influenced the sense of belonging of our participants, especially those in the third generation. It is very meaningful, given the South African context, that although this topic was not purposefully explored in the interviews, it still emerged as a subtext in some interviews when we analysed the data and reflected on their significance. Certainly more research should be conducted on this aspect. Furthermore, there should be research on those descendants of Italian immigrants who are not part of a "white" Italian community, and whose *italianità* might be very differently constructed, both in relation to Italy as a country of origin and to South Africa as a country of birth – people such as Don Mattera, quoted at the beginning of the study – whose family paths diverged from that of the dominant Italian community from which most of our (partially self-selected) participants came.

Unlike race, perhaps surprisingly to some readers, gender was not a focus in this study. Gender issues were not part of the initial research question, nor did they emerge as a theme from our interviews. It seems that participants' sense of belonging was not sufficiently strongly influenced by gender considerations for them to mention it. Our participants tended to speak of "family" or "parents" or "grandparents", and when only one side of the family was

Italian, the participants' sense of identity and belonging did not depend on whether it was the maternal or paternal side that was Italian. However, further research might explore the role of gender relations in second- and third-generation immigrants' experiences.

At the end of this specific research journey, we hope that this is indeed only the beginning of a longer personal and scholarly journey into the investigation of a diasporic group, Italians in South Africa, who have been ignored for too long, but which nevertheless have been living and negotiating their lives abroad without ever fully lose their connection with their native or ancestral land, Italy.

References

Gabaccia, D. R. (2000). *Italy's many diasporas*. University of Washington Press.

Marino, S. (2021). Thrown into the world: The shift between pavlova and pasta in the ethnic identity of Australians originating from Italy. *Journal of Sociology, 57*(2), 231–248. https://doi.org/10.1177/1440783319888283

Sala, E. (2017). *The Italian-ness is in the family: A critical evaluation of the role of family in constructions of ethnicity and connections to homeland among two cohorts of second generation Italian-Australians* [Doctoral dissertation, PhD Thesis, University of Western Australia]. https://api.research-repository.uwa.edu.au/ws/portalfiles/portal/20507794/THESIS_DOCTOR_OF_PHILOSOPHY_SALA_Emanuela_2017.pdf

Appendix
The participants

The participants' ages and occupations are given for the time of the interviews which took place between 2018 and 2020. Their situations may have altered since the study was done.

Gender identification is implied in the pronouns chosen.

Alberto was 24 years old. He was based in Johannesburg and studied engineering at the University of the Witwatersrand. Both his parents were born in South Africa. His grandparents migrated to South Africa after World War II – his paternal grandfather came from Segromigno in the Lucca province, and his paternal grandmother from Porcari, in the same province. Alberto's maternal grandfather came from Campobasso (Molise) and his maternal grandfather from Abruzzo.

Angelo was 18 years old. He was in his final year of high school at the time of the interview. His maternal grandparents came to South Africa from Rome after World War II. The decision was made on the advice of Angelo's grandfather's uncle, who had been a prisoner at Zonderwater. Angelo's father is an English-speaking South African.

Antonio was 24 years old. He was an industrial designer working in Johannesburg. His father was Italian, and his mother was Greek. His paternal grandfather was born in Albania, but towards the end of World War II, he fled to Italy, where he met Antonio's grandmother and they got married. Shortly thereafter, Antonio's father was born, in 1944, in the city of Bari in Puglia. Antonio's paternal grandparents moved to South Africa in 1946.

Barbara was 28 years old. She worked as a research intern in Cape Town. Her paternal grandparents came from Gattinara, in the province of Vercelli, and her maternal grandparents came from Buie, in Istria. Her parents were both born in Italy but moved to South Africa when they were very young.

Beatrice was 56 years old. She was single with no children and worked as a paramedic. Her mother came from Ivrea, in Torino. Her father came from Sardinia and worked for Olivetti. He met Beatrice's mother when he was on a training course in Ivrea, and they married by proxy.

Carla was 18 years old and was a third-year student. Her maternal grandmother was born in South Africa, but she was "raised Italian". Her maternal grandfather was born in Italy but came to South Africa after World War II at the age of 16. Her father was born in England.

Charles was 33 years old and single, with no children. He worked at a South African university. His mother was born in Lucca in Tuscany and moved to South Africa with her parents after World War II; Charles's father was an English-speaking South African.

Dario was 41 years old. He lived in Cape Town and was married with two small children. He worked in the motor industry. His father came to South Africa through Zambia and Zimbabwe. His paternal family came from North Sicily, and his maternal family from Rome.

Diego was 60 years old and is a second-generation Italian. He was divorced from his first wife, with whom he had three children, and he had remarried. He worked in real estate. His father came from Lecco and his mother from Marina di Carrara. His father first immigrated to Mozambique but moved to South Africa three years later. His parents were married by proxy.

Donatella was 47 years old. She worked in the financial services industry. She was married to an English-speaking South African and had a young son. Her maternal grandparents were from Naples and came to South Africa before World War II. They were married by proxy. Her father was born in Abruzzo and came to South Africa in 1964.

Federica was 19 years old, and a university student. Her mother's family came from Ireland, and her father's family from a small town outside Bologna. Her paternal grandparents came to South Africa during World War II, via Ethiopia, from a small town just outside of Bologna, San Giovanni, in Persiceto.

Fabrizio was 23 years old. Both his parents were born in South Africa, but all his grandparents came from Italy. His paternal grandparents came from Abruzzo to South Africa after World War II. His maternal grandfather came from Massa-Carrara (Tuscany) to South Africa on a mining contract. His maternal grandmother came from Bergamo, and her grandfather was a prisoner of war in South Africa who briefly went back to Italy after the war but then came back to South Africa.

Gabriella was in her twenties. She was a university student living in Johannesburg. Her mother was born in Rome; her father was born in South Africa, but his family moved to and from Italy over the years, until he turned 22 and married her mother in Italy. After they had Gabriella's brother, her parents decided to move to South Africa, because of a lack of facilities for her brother's special needs in Italy. Her maternal grandparents are still in Italy. Her parental grandparents came to South Africa after World War II but had passed away by the time of the study.

Giulia was 19 years old. Her mother was of Greek origin. Her father was born in South Africa. Her paternal grandfather was born in Caravaggio (Bergamo) and moved between Italy and Rhodesia (Zimbabwe), and eventually settled in South Africa. Her paternal grandmother was born in South Africa after her great-grandparents had immigrated from Torino.

Ignazio was 36 years old and was married. He worked in the property business. Both his parents were born in South Africa. His mother was Afrikaans-speaking. His Italian roots came from his father's side of the family – his paternal grandfather came from Terni (Umbria) and was in South Africa as a prisoner of war during World War II, initially at Zonderwater, then in Worcester.

Lilla was a university student in her early twenties, living in Johannesburg. The maternal side of her family originally came from Sicily, but her grandmother was born in Eritrea. Her mother was born in South Africa. Her paternal family originated from Piedmont, but her grandparents met in South Africa, and her father was born there.

Lara was 52 years old, married with one daughter. Lara ran an alternative health business. Her paternal grandparents came from Montepulciano in Tuscany, but her father came to South Africa from Italy after the war in the early 1950s. Her mother was a South African of Afrikaner descent.

Laura was 34 years old and single. Her father was born in Tanzania, as her paternal grandparents moved to Tanzania from Torino after World War II, and then to South Africa. Her mother was an English-speaking South African.

Marcelle was a 58-year-old woman, who was divorced but in a relationship at the time of the interview. She worked in real estate. Her father came from Trieste. Her grandfather was a prisoner of war in Worcester, but his wife and son (Marcelle's father), their only child, were in Italy during the war. Two years after the war ended, her grandfather came back to South Africa with his wife and young son but died soon after that from lung cancer. Marcelle's grandmother then married a South African man. During his travels to and fro between South Africa and Italy, Marcelle's father married Marcelle's mother, who was of Portuguese descent, in South Africa. They moved to Italy together.

Marina was 23 years old and a third-year university student. She is Tullio's daughter. She was single and lived with her parents and brother.

Matteo was 56 years old and was married to an English-speaking South African. They had two children. His father came to South Africa in the 1950s from Chieti (Abruzzo) on a three-year contract, but he stayed in the country for the remainder of his life. In 1957, Matteo's mother, his grandmother, and his uncle came to South Africa from the Abruzzo region. Since they were all from Abruzzo, the two families socialised together in South Africa and that was how Matteo's parents met.

Nadia was 40 years old. She was born in Pretoria and was married to an English-speaking South African. Her mother came from the United Kingdom and her father was from outside Avellino. Both her parents moved to South Africa in the mid-1960s and met in South Africa.

Nino was 28 years old. His father moved to South Africa from Torino after developing a skin condition which could be better managed in the South African climate. When he left Italy, he was already dating Nino's mother, who came from Padova. She came to South Africa to visit him and decided to move there permanently. They got married and had Nino and his brother.

Sandra was 35 years old, married with no children. Both her parents were of Italian origin, born in South Africa. They met in South Africa and their families were family friends. Her maternal grandfather, born in Rome, was a prisoner of war in Zonderwater, but after the war, he did not want to return to Italy and decided to stay in South Africa. Her maternal grandmother came to South Africa from Genova with a South African soldier after the war. They were married, but while travelling to visit family in Italy, she heard that her husband had died in an accident. Nevertheless, she decided to return to live in South Africa. As a widow she met Sandra's grandfather and they got married. Sandra's paternal grandparents also came from Genova.

Silvio was 36 years old and single. The maternal side of the family was of Dutch/French descent. The paternal side of the family was Italian and Polish. Silvio's paternal grandfather came from Bergamo.

Susanna, Sandra's sister, was 38 years old and was married to a South African man, with whom she had three children. Both her parents were born in South Africa.

Theodore was a 24-year-old single student. His father was born in South Africa from an Afrikaner background. His mother was born in South Africa, after Theodore's grandfather, who was born in Friuli, came to South Africa, escaping the war. His maternal great-grandfather was in the Zonderwater camp.

Tullio was 57 years old, married with one daughter and one son. He ran a property business. His father came from Bari and his mother from near Naples. His father immigrated to South Africa after seeing an advertisement in a newspaper about the free passage on a ship, board and lodging, and food, and a three-year contract in the mines, where he then worked. Tullio's maternal grandfather came via Cape Town on his way to Argentina and stayed a few weeks. He was in Argentina for six months, then went back to Italy, but eventually came back to South Africa, bringing his wife and children. Tullio's parents met in South Africa at the Italian Club.

Index

For Product Safety Concerns and Information please contact our EU
representative GPSR@taylorandfrancis.com
Taylor & Francis Verlag GmbH, Kaufingerstraße 24, 80331 München, Germany

www.ingramcontent.com/pod-product-compliance
Lightning Source LLC
Chambersburg PA
CBHW071748270326
41928CB00013B/2842